LOG
CABIN
CAMPFIRE
COOKIN'

Illustration By Cousin Salty "Sandra Vicars"

Index;

*" **Making Memories with Family & Friends are the best Reasons to go Camping.** "*

"PROTECTING OUR WORLD IS A JOB THAT REQUIRES ALL OF US."

Log Cabin Grub Cookbooks

900 East Carnation Drive   Tel (801) 571-0789
Sandy, Utah 84094   Fax (801) 523-6240

D1478025

Page 1

"NO Trace Camp Tips" Inside

" LOG CABIN CAMPFIRE COOKIN "

Well lets see,---I guess the best thing about Campfire Cookin is the opportunity of families to be together in the out-of -doors and share the taste of that great outdoor cooking. Not to mention the physical exercise you get traveling around the campfire trying to stay out of the smoke. We hope you will read our book and enjoy the hints, gadgets, stories and Recipes that we are sharing with you. Whether you sleep under the stars, in a tent, or bring along a metal tent (campers & motor homes), your camping trips should be relaxing and full of good memories. Future camp trips usually include conversations about past experiences that left a memory worth sharing over and over. Record in a journal or diary all the fun things you do in order to be able to share them with your children when they are grown. I always tried to take pictures and include them with the memories. A lot of THANKS goes to my Mom & Dad for the great times we had as kids on camping, fishing and hunting trips. I classify my Mom as one of the best camp cooks ever. We usually had a few relatives or friends along on our camp trips, and the "Charles Oscar Dunn" family was one of them. They were great people and became adopted Uncle, Aunt and cousins. My Dad & uncle Oscar were in Scouts together for over 30 years. Their love for the out-of-doors was taught to us every where we went. My love for the Native American way of life and 35 plus years in Scouting have only enhanced my love for the out of doors. It is a privilege to use our Parks and Natural Resources and I hope to be able to share that belief with others. Throughout this book you will get suggestions from the NOLS school, "National Outdoor Leadership School" and LNT (Leave no Trace) Also, a lot of tips on camping from the " **NINE MILE HISTORIC RANGER STATION** "in Missoula Mt. to help us preserve our out of doors

Page 2

" Lets talk about Vinegar"

Vinegar is one of the items I always take with me when I leave home. **NATURAL APPLE CIDER VINEGAR** , that is. I mix the vinegar in a spray bottle at a 4 to 1 mixture. 4 water, 1 vinegar. It serves as a tenderizer and a disinfectant. And, as you know, anything tender cooks faster. Spraying the vinegar solution on meats and vegetables will kill all the bacteria that forms at room temperature. Spraying it on your pots, will disinfect them and make them easier to clean. Spraying it on your hands, and on the cooking surface you use is also a safe way to go.

Taking a spray bottle of vinegar with you when you go camping, is a good idea also. It's a disinfectant for cuts, scrapes and bites. You can treat sunburns by spraying them lightly every few minutes to cool the burn and let the heat out. I don't know about your camp trips, but my 5 kids had their share of accidents. When my son Steve fell 20 feet through the quakie branches and ran a branch thru his hand, the vinegar water helped to keep the infection out and allowed it to heal.

One time Justin, one of my twins, got a fish hook in his finger and we had to freeze it to get it out. Another time one was imbedded so far in we had to take him into Pinedale to have it removed. A dentist was the only one available, and right after he finished a root canal on his dog, he helped Justin. By soaking the hand and keeping the wound disinfected and the skin tender, it allowed the hand to heal with no scar. Soaking sore tired feet in warm vinegar water mixed 3 to 1 helps to relax the muscles and relieve the ache. Soaking feet helps to remove calluses and soften skin so that blisters won't form Soaking hands in warm vinegar water, softens skin and removes hang nails. It also keeps infections out of rose bush scratches and cactus stings. Vinegar is available in most stores. I take a tbsp. of vinegar in a little water every morning to help tenderize my joints and give me energy. It helps to relieve the arthritis pain in my hands. Vinegar kills bacteria in water, so ------ it's a good thing to take camping. Use it in your rinse water for dishes. Make VINEGAR a household word in your home, "The pioneers did."

" LOOK FOR NO TRACE CAMPING TIPS THROUGHOUT THIS BOOK. "

VINEGAR CONTINUED:

Apple cider vinegar is a marvelous combination of tart good taste and germ killing acids. It is fermented from sweet apple cider and takes its color from the tannins which flow from the ruptured cell walls of ripe apples. Apple Cider Vinegar contains more than thirty important nutrients, a dozen minerals, over a dozen vitamins and essential acids and several enzymes. Plus, it has a large dose of pectin for a healthy heart. Apple vinegar with sweet energy laden honey, is a supportive measure that encourages the body to defend itself from sickness. This combination can be used to help lower cholesterol. And, vinegar is said to shift the body's gears into low. Protecting us from stress related illness. A stronger dose of vinegar and honey (2 tbsp. vin. 2 tbsp. honey) in a glass of water and taken every morning is proven to lower cholesterol and normalize blood pressure. Through the ages, vinegar and honey has been prescribed as an aid in maintaining good general health, controlling diseases such as arthritis, and controlling weight. Both honey and vinegar contain large amounts of potassium. Neither are considered a drug, but are pure natural foods that promote the body's ability to help itself. Drinking a glass of water with 2 tsp. of vinegar and honey curb's the appetite before a meal and promotes good health. New research is beginning to show the wonderful effects or Vinegar and Honey. For good health and general well being, try vinegar and honey.

" <u>Simmer ½ cup vinegar in a pot of water to sweeten the air and absorb the odors indoors.</u>

" <u>Good common judgment in all outdoor activities is the key to a successful camp.</u>"

<u>NOLS—National Outdoor Leadership School was founded in 1965. Their mission is to be the best source and teacher of wilderness skills that protect the environment and users.</u>
Find them at 288 main street, Lander, Wyo. 82520   http://www.nols.edu/

ALL ABOUT THE BOOK

Since I have been involved with the NO-TRACE Camp Schools in Missoula Mt., at the **Nine Mile Historic Ranger Station**, I cannot believe how my awareness of the wilderness has improved. I am conscious more than ever of how people treat the out of doors. I try to encourage my Dutch Oven classes to get involved and show others how to care for our resources. The Rangers and teachers of the personnel that represent the KNOL'Ss program as very special people and know their stuff. The Scouting programs stress the importance of this way of life in the back country, but a little help from all my friends that read this book would help to make our outdoor experiences worth having. Do your part to help keep our country clean, and if your ever near Missoula, Mt.. be sure to drop in and see the **Historic 9-Mile Ranger Station** and take the tour. Tell them Colleen sent you and they'll probably say "WHO ". Just kidding.

ABOUT the Cookbook Layout;

The book was designed with the average camper in mind. The recipes have been placed head to head in order for the book to be read in a standing position. This makes the book more readable when you are changing pages. A campfire cookbook is usually hung from the cook box or over a tree branch. There is hardly ever a place to lay it flat.

CAST-IRON HISTORY

Early reference to the Black pots can be found in the old testament as Cauldron cooking. It is referred to as early as 4000 BC. Reports of Columbus coming to America also brought Black Pots to our attention. An early Oxford Dictionary, said that " pot ", is the name given to a vessel that grows narrower towards the top, and " kettle" to the vessel that grows wider up top. A pot will except a lid easier that a Kettle. Shakespeare in about 1606, referred to boiling kettles and cauldrons in the witches scene of Macbeth. In 1620, when the pilgrims landed in Plymouth aboard the Mayflower, they were reported as cooking with the pots as they traveled. They built fires in sand pits and suspended the pots from the ships beams. This was easier than the stationary base supported pots, because the contents would slosh around with the sea movements. On real windy days, cooking would be suspended.

Until the start of the 18th century, iron was cast in baked loam or clay soil. This made for a rough surface and the mold generally broke after one casting. For many years, foundries were more advanced in the Holland area, and cast iron pots were imported to Britain. These early pots were very thick walled. In 1704, Abraham Darby traveled to Holland to inspect the foundries of Holland. From this trip the sand molds were perfected. In 1708, he received a patent for the process and soon after began to produce large quantities of cast iron pot in the furnace at Coalbrookdale. By the mid-eighteenth century, these pots were being shipped to the Americas. This joint venture with the Dutch pots resulted in the trading of pot salesmen throughout the colonies. When a trader was seen coming in his wagon, it was said, " Here comes the Dutchman with his ovens. Some were called Dinner pots, Gypsy pots, Bean pots, Stew pots and stock pots. By the late 1700's pots were being made in the American colonies also. Improvements came with a good lid and a flared edge to hold the coals on top. Some things have changed with the ovens but we still have an excellent cooking and browning pot that is very useful today. Cooking with the ovens and not lifting the lids will maintain 80 % or more of the food value. These ovens are really a self timing pot. Learning to judge your heats and waiting for the smell will tell you when it's done.

Care and Storing of your Oven

When storing your oven, be sure that it has been wiped out and it will be in a dry place. I place a single paper towel inside to make sure that any moisture that forms will be absorbed by the paper towel. If rust forms in your pot, simply scour it out with a SOS type pad and re-grease it before you cook in it again. As it cooks, it will re-season itself. Seasoning the oven can cause an odor in your home if you have not scrubbed of the protective coating. Always wipe out the excess oil with a dry paper towel before storing. It is now ready to use, when you need it next time. Be sure to heat your oven and lightly grease it before you use it again. If mine have gotten dusty are dirty, I will spray them with Vinegar water and wipe them out to disinfect them before I heat and grease them.

Sometimes when you do not use your oven for a while, it becomes rancid. That is easily detected by the spoiled smell of the pot when opened. The grease actually goes rather yellow looks like a gummy texture. Simply fill your oven with water, add a cup of apple cider Vinegar and boil; for a 1/2 hour on the stove. Remove and dump out water. You should be able to scrape or scour out the rancid grease and then lightly re-grease or oil while it is hot, and turn it upside down in a hot (400 or better) oven on a cookie sheet or on your Volcano with 15 briquettes.   If you have the storage bags they are nice to keep you ovens clean. You can also use Gunny sacks, paper bags or canvas covers, but I do not suggest plastic because it will make your oven sweat and cause rust.

If your oven gets real rusty or you have a chance to pick one up at a garage sale that is real rusty, you can have them Sand Blasted for around $2.00. Just look in the yellow pages of your phone book under sand blasting. Everyone has their secrets and you need to practice with your oven and do what suits you best. The more you try the better it will get. Like **Mama** used to say, "Practice will make Perfection Happen". **Your Dutch Oven will be your best friend if you use it.**

Judging the right temperature

There are a few important things to remember about a **Dutch Oven**. The 2/3rds rule is one of them and applies to every size.

BAKING: When using the Black Pot to bake in, the heat must be distributed on the top and bottom to maintain the proper temperature. Usually a 350 to 375 temp. is sufficient to bake most any dish. If you are in the wind it will take away some of your heat, but the following chart should help. You can raise or lower the temp by adding 1 briquette for every 18 to 20 degrees you wish to add to the cooking temperature.

Cooking with Briquets

OVEN SIZE	8"	10"	12"	14"	16"	22"
Top Heat(size + 3)	11	13	15	17	19	25

Oven size is 12" and add 3 briquettes you should have 350/375 degrees for about 25-30 minutes cooking.

In your Volcano, 10 Briquettes with no top heat will keep your oven at 350 to 375 using the damper.

OVEN SIZE	8"	10"	12"	14"	16"	22"
Bottom Heat (deduct 3)	5	7	9	11	13	19

When you are 2/3rds of the way through the baking recipe, remove the bottom heat except for 3 or 4 briquettes and this will prevent burning your food. The briquettes can be added to the top if necessary. If the top is browning to fast, remove 3 or 4 briquettes from the lid and allow baking to finish its time. Arranging the briquettes so that the heat remains even is also very important. Too much heat on one side will burn that spot and leave the middle doughy-done. Baking can be alot of fun in a Dutch Oven but proper heat and the 2/3rds rule are important factors.
Remember, that 350 degrees plus 3 full size briquettes will equal 375 degrees.

Page 6

CLEANING YOUR OVEN

On page 4 we briefly touched on the care of your oven. Alot of people will tell you never to wash the insides of your pot with soap, but I have found on occasion that I have had too. I have a pot of my Dads that is over 55 years old and it has been washed several times. It has no legs and today still cooks as good as any of my brand new ones. These pots are not very fragile, but still require a certain amount of care. Dropping them or banging them against a hard surface could crack them and then there ability to hold heat diminishes.

When you wash a pot, always have it at room temperature to avoid any problems. Use only a mild detergent and always rinse thoroughly. It is important to heat your pan and thoroughly dry it before storing I always clean my pans hot because it helps to release the food particles. I find it helpful to return the pot to the heat after emptying it, and spraying in a little Vinegar water to soften the food. Then I wipe it clean with paper towels and immediately lightly replace the protective grease coating that keeps the seasoning process going. Always wipe out the excess grease with a clean paper towel. Store the pots in a dry place with a clean sheet of paper towel inside to keep the moisture from rusting your oven. You take care of them and they'll do you proud. The 1 part vinegar & 4 parts water is a great cleaning agent and disinfectant. The Apple Cider Vinegar is something I learned from my Pioneer Grandparents and mom.

SEASONING YOUR DUTCH OVEN

Well, you just bought your first **Dutch Oven** and now your gona take it home. As your leaving the store, the salesperson tells you to be sure to season it before you use it. Oh boy, your thinking, what does that mean ?

If you ask 100 people how to season a **Dutch Oven**, you'll probably get 15 different answers. Most Dutch Ovens today are coated with a protective substance by the manufacturer. If it's Lodge, it will be a Laquer of some sort. You will need to heat the oven and scrub it in warm soapy water.. Rinse it thoroughly with **HOT** water. Place on the stove and heat it to evaporate the moisture and thoroughly dry it. Then, lightly grease it. Put it back in your regular oven, on your barbecue outside, on a Camp Chef or on your VOLCANO outdoor stove with 25 briquettes and bake it at 450 degrees or more until it is black.. All this does is bake protective grease coating into the pot and virtually give your pot a no-scrub surface. If the pot appears to be sticky, you have not baked it long or hot enough to burn the oil into the metal. . After 1 hour, you can let the oven cool down and give it another coat of oil if it is not covered well enough. You can return to the heat and bake it more. Be sure to turn the oven upside down so grease does not puddle up in the bottom.

If your pot is seasoned well and used often, you will find it very easy to clean. If my pots are cleaned while they are hot, they can almost be wiped out with VINEGAR water and virtually no scraping. I mix my Vinegar 1 part V. to 4 parts Water and keep it in a spray bottle. in my food box. Vinegar is a great disinfectant and a natural Tenderizer for all foods. After most dishes, you should be able to wipe out your Cast Iron with a paper towel to clean it. Never use margarine or butter to season your pot. Any oil or shortening will do. I love the taste of Bacon, so I use a **real light** coat of bacon grease.

MAIN DISHES AND BREAKFAST

Campfire Main Meals and Breakfasts

**Carry Along Pancake Mix (enough for 4 people for 3 meals)   *"This Recipe is very Versitile"*

6 cups wheat or white flour
1 full cup powdered milk   *Powdered Buttermilk works well-*
2 Tbsps. Baking powder
1 Tbsps. Salt

Mix all dry ingredients together and carry in a tightly covered container. When ready to use, add 2 cups water, 2 eggs, and 2 tbsp. oil to 2 1/3 cups flour mix. op
(Add 7-up, cream soda tonic water or ? in place of water.)
(2 tbsp. powdered eggs can be added to dry mix and omit fresh eggs.)

** Chuck Wagon Scrambled Eggs

Heat and lightly oil a cast iron fry pan. Stir in 1 cup canned tomatoes and 1 cup canned corn. Fresh tomatoes and corn can be used in season. Heat and add 6 eggs to the mixture. Stir to break the yolks and season with 1 heaping tsp. of Log Cabin Seasoning or your favorite seasoning. (Salt and Pepper will do)

VARIATIONS… Add mushrooms, Bacon bits, Ham pieces, Sausage, Hamburger, Salsa or Cheese. This can be served with a cornbread side dish or biscuits. Use your imagination and serve anything that sounds good to you. Breakfast is a very important meal, because it helps start your system for the day.

Try this same recipe in a Dutch Oven, over coals or campfire or in your oven at home. After adding the eggs, put the baking powder biscuits on top and sprinkle with seasoning lightly and sprinkle on cheese. Bake for 15 minutes, covered, or wait for the smell.

Pioneer Griddle Cakes

Pour 1 cup boiling water over ¾ cup cornmeal and stir until thick. Add 1 cup sour milk or buttermilk and 1 tbsp. molasses. Mix well and add 2 eggs, 1-1/2 tsp Real salt, 3 tbsp. oil or bacon grease, mix and add 1-1/2 cups flour and ¼ tsp. soda.

These pancakes can be changed by adding a variation of fruit, nuts, meats or cheeses. Even a can of tomatoes drained corn or left-over rice would be a variety. Serve with jellies, jam or syrups.

** Campfire Cowboy Potatoes

In the bottom of an 8" Dutch Oven, mash out a ½ lb. of sausage in a large patty. Layer 3 washed and sliced potatoes and 1 small onion, on top of the patty.. Spray with your vinegar water 6 or 8 times, sprinkle with Real salt and pepper, or 1 tsp of Log Cabin Seasoning. Cover and place on 6 briquettes in your Junior Volcano for 35 minutes or until you can see the moisture escape and smell it. Remove lid and add 1 cup cheese white and yellow mixed. Let set for 3 to 4 minutes to melt cheese. If you want to put biscuits on top, do so as soon as you get the first smell and return to the heat for 10 to 12 minutes. If cooking on the campfire, brush back the coals and set D.O. on the ground. Shovel coals around the outside and allow to cook till you can smell it. If using briquettes only, 6 on the bottom and 11 on the top. You may have to add more briquettes to finish cooking. You can also cook this in your home oven. ENJOY

** Campfire Mushroom Burgers

2 lbs. Hamburger
3 medium onions, sliced
1 can cream mushroom or celery
2 cups sliced mushrooms, canned or fresh.
1/8 tsp. Nutmeg
1 tbsp. Log Cabin Seasoning
1 can French fried onions. (optional)
8 big buns or 2 loaves French Bread sliced.

De---licious

" There's some fish recipes in with the veggies!!

Worth Slappin your wings over

In the bottom of a warmed and oiled, 12 inch Dutch Oven, crumble the hamburger and fry. Stir often to break apart and add, Nutmeg, seasoning , Real salt and pepper if you wish. Add the Mushrooms and stir until cooked. Add the soup and simmer while you place the buns or bread on a plate as an open face sandwich. Place sliced onion on bun and put a heaping spoon full on the onion and bread. Crumble the French fried onions on top of the hamburger mixture and serve open face or with a top. This dish can be made on a Volcano, a propane stove a campfire, or at home.

VARIATIONS.   Add chopped olives, green or red peppers, sliced tomatoes, stewed tomatoes, green chilies, ,grated cheese, bacon bits or any thing else that sounds good.

Wilderness use continues to grow at an astonishing rate, making it more imperative than ever to " Walk a Soft Path". " Tread Lightly".

**Celery Chicken Legs and Thyme

10 drum sticks (thighs) rolled in flour
¼ tsp. black pepper
1 tsp Real salt
6 potatoes washed for slicing
½ cup flour.

½ tsp celery salt
½ tsp. thyme
½ tsp. marjoram
¼ cup oil

Mix flour and seasonings together well. Spray chicken with vinegar water solution and roll in flour mixture. Into a warmed and oiled Dutch Oven, place the floured chicken, browning in the ¼ cup oil. Arrange the chicken in the bottom of the Dutch Oven and cover with Potato slices. Cover the oven and allow to bake on 12 briquettes in the Volcano, or 10 on the bottom and 15 on top in the open air. Add more as needed in the open. In your oven at home, bake for 45 to 50 minutes. ..If carrots are added, do at the same time you put in potatoes. Carrots are the hardest vegetable to cook. Celery can be added with potatoes also.   For a one pot dish, add biscuits after you first smell it and return to the heat source 15 minutes more.

In Yellowstone National Park, users must obtain a permit before hiking into the back country and campsites are designated. Only 7 parties a day are allowed to travel Idaho's middle fork of the Salmon River.

Renew old sponges by washing them in soapy water to which a little vinegar has been added. Soak over night in a vinegar solution. Enough to cover the sponge.

Page 10

** Beef Roast and Chuckwagon Veggies

3 or 4 lb. Beef or Pork Roast ------------3 tbsp. flour------------4 tsp. Beef bouillon------------1/4 cup oil------
1 cup water-----------1 cup buttermilk or powdered milk------------2 tbsp. Log Cabin Seasoning-------------
or ½ tsp. thyme, onion salt, garlic salt, Real salt, Pepper, paprika and rosemary----------5 potatoes and
carrots sliced in half-----------2 medium onions quartered-----------2 cups broccoli and 2 cups cauliflower.

Warm and oil a 12 inch Dutch Oven (deep or shallow). Place the Roast in the Dutch oven, on a trivet if
it's a deep oven, and spray with vinegar water. # # Sprinkle the roast with the seasoning. Cover and
place on heat. 12 Briquettes in a Volcano, 15 on top and 10 on the bottom for briquettes only. Campfire
procedure on page 6. In a fry pan with 2 tbsp. oil, put the flour in and stir until brown. Add water,
buttermilk, beef bullion and any of the spices you desire. Cook until mixture thickens. Prepare veggies
and after roast has cooked for ½ hour,--------lift lid and add carrots, onions and potatoes. around the meat.
Spoon the gravy over the top and bake until you smell it. About 1 hour and 10 minutes. Lift the lid and
place the cauliflower and broccoli on top. Replace lid and cook for another 15 minutes.
Mix vinegar and water in 4 to 1 solution, as discussed on page 3.

Goo------ood

**If it takes you longer to cook your recipes, maybe your lifting the lid to much or using inexpensive
briquettes. If it's windy wrap your ovens with tin foil when cooking in the open.**

**The belief is that most damage to wildlands is the result of lack of education, not
malice. Most back country users are caring , intelligent people who want to do
the right thing.**

*** Ranch Hand Ham Pot Pie

"Don't pass this one up."

"ooo---e"

3 cups chopped cut up ham
2 cans cheddar cheese soup—mixed
3 cups chopped broccoli
½ cup broken pieces of spaghetti, uncooked
2 cups basic baking mix (page 40 Log Cabin Grub)
1 cup milk or 7-up------2 eggs
1 heaping tbsp mustard

     In a warm and oiled 12 inch Dutch oven, combine the ham, soup, broccoli and spaghetti. Bring to a low simmering boil over the heat. In a bowl, combine the baking mix, milk and mustard. Pour over the top of the ham mixture. Bake in your oven on 350 for 35 minutes, In a Volcano on 12 briquettes and wait for the smell. (about 30 to 35 minutes.)   On a propane stove turn fire to low and place 10 or 12 briquettes on top. Briquettes only, start with 15 on top and 10 on bottom, add as needed. to maintain heat.

REMOVING RUST; Place rusty pot in a pot that is larger and stuff around the sides and inside the pot with alfalfa   Hay (fresh or dry doesn't matter) Fill with enough water to cover the pot and add 1 cup Apple Cider Vinegar. Let sit for and hour or heat on the stove for 20 minutes and rust will disappear. Rhubarb leaves will work also but not as fast.. Remove from solution, scrub with SOS pad and rinse well. Put on the heat or in the oven and heat well to dry all moisture. Re-season.

**Are you a WOODSY OWL and a SMOKEY BEAR in the back country??????.
Help us all keep our wilderness for future generations.**

** Breakfast Potato Boats

8 left-over or freshly baked potatoes
2 cups grated cheese
2 lb. Bacon cooked and crumbled
½ tsp. Real salt and ¼ tsp pepper

½ cup butter or margarine
¼ cup chopped onions
2 tsp. Log Cabin seasoning
1 tsp. paprika

"So fun to Do."

Make a cut in the top of the potatoes and scoop out all the insides. Or, make 8 potato boats out of tin foil and use mashed potatoes. Mix all ingredients except 1 tsp. seasoning or paprika. Spoon mix back into potato and bake in a 12 inch Dutch oven that has been warmed and lightly oiled. 30 minutes on 10 to 12 briquettes in your Volcano, 10 briquettes on the bottom and 15 on top for out door cookin, on a propane fire very low with 10 briquettes on top. Remove lid and put grated cheese on top and bacon bits on top if desired and serve with bacon hot rolls or pancakes. **The same dish can be done with sausage or ham.**

** Hamburger Fry Pan Breakfast.

Warm and lightly grease a 12 inch fry pan. Crumble 1-1/2 lbs. of good hamburger in the bottom and cook thru. Break into small pieces. Add 2 lb. pkg. of hash browns or 4 cups. Stir until heated thru and break 6 eggs over the top. Cover with lid or tin foil and steam for 5 to 6 minutes. Check to see if your eggs are the way you like them. Season to taste and sprinkle with cheese if you like. White cheese is very good. Serve with hot biscuits or pancakes. This is good with sausage or crumbled bacon also Log Cabin seasoning or salsa is an option to use also.

__Plan ahead and know your area before you go camping. Check your weather, plan the right clothes know your fire plan for cooking, check the trails and terrain and know the nearest contact station in the area.__

** Beans and Sausage Breakfast

2 lbs. country sausage
4 cans different kinds of beans
(kidney-northern-pinto & etc.)
2 tsp. mustard

1 medium onion chopped
1 cup ketchup or salsa
½ cup brown sugar
1 chopped green or red pepper

"What a way to start the morning"

In a 10 or 12 inch skillet or the bottom of a 12 inch Dutch oven, brown the sausage and onion. Drain off most of the grease and add the drained beans and pepper. Add remaining ingredients and simmer for 30 minutes or so. Serve over hashbrowns , scrambled eggs, biscuits. or toast. Great dish for breakfast or supper, add pork and beans if you like. Serves 10 or more people. Don't be afraid to experiment and add eggs or hashbrowns to the mixture as it simmers. 12 briquettes in a Volcano, 10 on the bottom and 15 on top if briquettes only, and the campfire method on page 6. Can be done in your oven at 350 degrees.

** Bunkhouse Rice Breakfast

1 cup sliced celery
3 tbsp. butter
1 cup chopped mushrooms
12 eggs
2 tbsp. Log Cabin Seasoning

1 cup chopped green peppers
1 small onion chopped
4 cups minute rice or left-overs
1 cup milk
or Real Salt & pepper to taste

"Giddy-up" & Go

In a large skillet or a 12 inch Dutch oven, sauté the first 5 ingredients. Combine the egg, milk and seasonings—pour over the vegetables. Stir in the rice just enough the separate. Cover and cook over low heat until eggs are set up. About 20 minutes.

**One Pot Sausage Toast

8-10 slices of bread
1-1/2 lbs. of cooked, drained sausage
1 lb. Grated cheese
6 eggs
3 cups milk
½ cup sliced mushrooms
½ tsp. Real salt and nutmeg
1 tsp. cinnamon

"The Family comes to Breakfast"

Warm and grease your 12 inch Dutch oven or a large skillet. Bread slices can be placed in the pot whole or broken in pieces. Spread sausage and mushrooms over bread pieces. Mix eggs, milk, cinnamon and nutmeg together and pour on bread. Allow to sit for 5 minutes with a lid on, and return to the heat. 10 to 12 briquettes in you Volcano, 10 bottom and 12 top for briquettes only, low heat on stove top. In your oven 350 degrees until you can smell it. About 30 minutes. Sprinkle cheese on top just before you serve and cover for 3 to 5 minutes. Serve with syrup, jam honey or etc. Serves 7 to 10 people. Cheese can be omitted. Bacon can be crumbled on top. Substitute ham also if you want a different taste.

A splash of Apple Cider vinegar can be added to your rinse water when camping or at home to kill germs and stop water spots.

On most popular rivers, camping is restricted to a few highly impacted areas. Never camp right on the water. Obey the regulations.

Cowtown All Day Breakfast

Oft times in the west, a breakfast had to last you all day long. So---the camp cook would feed the wranglers a hearty meal to last them till supper. The following is one of those breakfasts.

¼ cup bacon grease or shortening
6 medium potatoes, washed and sliced
1 large sliced onion
2 Tbsps. Log Cabin Seasoning or Real salt and pepper to taste
1 cup diced ham, or fried bacon or sausage   8 eggs
Melt grease in a large fry pan or the bottom of a 12 inch Dutch oven. Add the onions, potatoes and seasonings. Cook till tender. Break the eggs over the potatoes and pour the meat on top. Cover and cook for 7 to 10 minutes. Spoon on plates or cut in pie like wedges. Follow previous cooking instructions.

Variations;
1.   Grated cheese over the top just before serving.
2.   Salsa and sour cream on to for a zesty flavor.
3.   Add green and yellow or red peppers
4.   1 can mushroom soup mixed with the eggs.
5.   Hamburger used for a hearty beef meal
6.   Kidney or pinto beans mixed with the potatoes.

Don't forget the cheese -- It's the Best part"

<u>**All of us who enjoy the out-of-doors must also take the responsibility of the human impact and do our best to do our part of cleaning and repairing after any activity.**</u>

** Sausage and Biscuits Log Cabin Style

1 lb. Country sausage	2 pkg. refrigerated biscuits (or 12 precooked)
½ tsp. sage	2 tsp. Log cabin Seasoning
¼ tsp. ginger	10 to 20 slices of white or yellow cheese

Bake biscuits in 12 inch Dutch oven. Butter tops and sprinkle with seasoning. Slice in half. Mix seasonings with sausage and fry up in small patties. Place sausage on biscuits and add 1 slice of cheese. Place on top roll and return to the pan for 2 to 3 minutes to allow cheese to melt. Scrambled or hard fried eggs can be added to the sandwich.

Wipe down cutting boards and counter surfaces with full strength Vinegar, it cleans, cuts grease, absorbs odors and disinfects.

** Shepherds Breakfast

" Mouth Watering "

In a large cast iron skillet or a 12 inch Dutch oven, cook 1 lb. Bacon and drain off excess fat. Add 1 pkg. of frozen hashbrowns and cook on low medium heat for about 7 to 10 minutes. Turning when brown. Make 8 wells in the potatoes and break an egg in each. Sprinkle lightly with Real salt and pepper or Log cabin seasoning. Cover and cook long enough to set the eggs. Cheese can be added if desired. Serve with hot breakfast rolls.

A shortage of Potassium and iron in the diet can make your ears ring. Sweet Potatoes and Yams are a great source to replace it in your diet. Not to mention the Vitamin A. Cooking in Cast Iron also adds iron to your diet.

Page 17

** Southwestern Cowboy Omelet

1 cup chopped ham
8 eggs beaten with ¼ cup milk
1 small jalapeno pepper minced.
1 onion, 1 ripe avocado, chopped
½ tsp. Real salt and pepper

1 cup shredded white cheese
1 tbsp. oil
8 or 10 strips of bacon, fried and chopped
1 tomato, chopped
½ cup salsa (optional)

" mushrooms" or green peppers sure add to this one

Sauté onion and pepper in large skillet until tender. Remove from grease and set aside. Pour beaten eggs into the skillet, cover and cook for 3 to 5 minutes. Mix together onion, avocados, tomatoes, bacon and ½ the cheese. Spread over the eggs and fold over. Sprinkle remaining cheese over the top of omelet and season. Cover and cook for 3 minutes or until cheese is melted. Top with salsa and sour cream if desired. Cut in slices and serve with rolls or tortillas.

We could learn a lot from the weather, it pays absolutely no mind to criticism.

You can preach a better sermon with your life than your lips.

** Danish Schmarren

Warm a cast iron skillet , oil it well enough to cover the bottom and place 4 cups milk in a bowl with ¼ cup water. Add 6 eggs beat well, and add 2 cups flour, dash of salt. Mix well. When oil is hot, add the batter stirring well as it cooks to break apart as a hot cake. When cooked thru and lightly brown, serve with syrup or jam. Cinnamon, Nutmeg or both can be added to the milk.

** Meat Stuffed Sandwich

THIS IS A QUICK RECIPE FOR OUTDOOR COOKIN.
2 tbsp. butter or margarine
2 cups chopped ham, bacon, sausage or hamburger
3 cups shredded white, yellow or both cheese
3 cups broccoli and 1 medium onion chopped
2 loaves of bread dough, frozen or freshly made

Fast - Fun to do & Good Tastin

Roll out each loaf of bread in an oblong shape, butter the tops and spread ½ of each ingredient on the dough. Roll the dough up from the sides and fold in the end piece to make a bread loaf that will fit in a 12 inch Dutch Oven. Warm and grease the oven and place the rolled dough inside. It can be in a ring or side by side. Lightly butter the top and sprinkle with paprika or Log cabin seasoning. Allow the dough to rise for 20 to 25 minutes, covered. Place 3 or 4 briquettes on top to speed up the process. Bake at 350 until you can smell it which should be about 35 minutes. Remember the Dutch oven will tell you when it is done by the smell. In the Volcano use 12 briquettes on the bottom in a circle. In the open 10 on the bottom and 15 on top. When done, sprinkle with cheese and let sit long enough to melt. A can of cream soup can be added to the mix to add a gravy and more moisture. Cheddar cheese, cream broccoli, cream celery or mushroom to name a few.

Do not try to rush when baking in a Dutch oven, you will surely burn the bottom. - *No Heat in the middle*

If you get into real deep water, be sure to keep your mouth shut.

** Granny's Breakfast Gravy

½ cup margarine or butter
3 tbsp. flour
½ tsp. Real salt
1/8 tsp. pepper
2 ½ cup milk
1/8 tsp. onion salt
Dash of Garlic, optional
6 hard boiled eggs, peeled and chopped.

Warm and lightly grease a 10 inch Dutch oven. Put butter in the bottom and melt, stir in flour and seasoning . Add milk. This will make a creamy white sauce gravy. Simmer slowly until thick, add chopped eggs. This can be served over biscuits, toast or what ever. Sausage, ham or bacon can be added to the gravy with the eggs. This recipe can be doubled very easily. Feeds 6 people.
VARIATIONS: Add mushrooms, green peppers, green onions, broccoli, cheese or etc. Before adding meats, be sure they are cooked.

You have to do your own growing, no matter how tall your father was. Swallow your pride occasionally, it really isn't fattening.

Most of the damage done to the Wilderness areas and back country, is due to a lack of education. Most users want to do the right thing, but good intentions are not enough.
You are just one person, but one person can begin to make a difference.
You can do something.

** Ole' Burger Casserole

2 lbs. of hamburger cooked with 1 medium onion and 1 chopped green pepper. This can be done in the bottom of a 12 inch Dutch oven or large fry pan that has been warmed and oiled. Add 1 large can of stewed tomatoes and 1 large can of tomato sauce. Simmer and add 1 pkg. of dry Taco seasoning. Cut 1 large pkg. of tortillas into small chunks. 24 small—18 large. Add all but 2 hands full to mix. Add 2 cans kidney beans to hamburger mix. Simmer long enough to warm thru. Mix an 8 oz. Pkg. of sour cream and a 16 oz. Pkg. of cottage cheese together in a bowl. With your spoon, make openings in the hamburger mixture. Drop cream mixture into the spoon wells. Cover the top of mixture with tortillas, cheese and black olives. Cover and bake enough to warm thru and melt cheese. About 15 to 18 minutes. { A mild jar of Salsa can be added in place of stewed tomatoes.}

It's not your position that makes you happy, but your disposition.

Learn to laugh at your self, you'll have a life long source of amusement.

Please Help me I Love to Laugh + make others Happy "

When meeting a horse party, move off the foot path and stand quietly until they pass so s not to startle the horses. If can be a real safety factor for all. Select a route that avoids fragile areas or wet lands. When passing others, try not to walk on the plants and widen the trail. Pass with care or stop to let others pass.

** Cowpuncher Omelet

2 cups mushrooms
1 cup grated cheese
2 tbsp. oil, margarine or butter
1-1/2 cups milk

2 cups ham, diced
1 dozen eggs
2 medium onions sliced
1 cup chopped green pepper

Ridin' the Range couldn't Be Better

Melt oil in warmed Dutch Oven. Sauté onions, green peppers and mushrooms until clear in color. Add ham and warm thru. Whip eggs in a bowl with milk and add a tsp. of soda. Pour over the vegetables and top with a cup of grated cheese. Cover and bake on 12 briquettes in your Volcano, or 10 briquettes on the bottom and 15 on top. In a campfire remember to brush back the coals and place the Dutch oven on the ground. Pile coals about 2/3 of the way up the sides of the oven, and wait for the smell. Should take about 2o to 25 minutes.

Cooking and camping in the outdoors has long been a real pleasure for most people in the USA. Naturally this attitude is carried to the back yard cooking area. There are many State and National Parks that offer a great place to stay and enjoy the sights and sounds of the open world around us. Study birds, listen to the winds, smell the flowers, observe the clouds, and do a little rock hunting to get to know your out of doors. The out of doors can be a college of knowledge to those willing to learn about the world around you. Outdoor eating is immensely popular, do your best to make it easy and enjoyable. Simple one pot meals in a Dutch oven can make your camp trip enjoyable. The Volcano stove is like owning your own portable fire pit.

If you do meet other hikers on the trail, move off to one side and stop, continuing to walk only widens the trail. When meeting horses, remain still and speak softly as horses can startle easily.

***Cow Camp Enchiladas

1 large onion chopped
1 medium can chopped olives.
1-1/2 lbs. hamburger
2 cups grated cheddar cheese
10 tortillas shells
1 small can green chilies
1 medium can enchilada sauce
1 can cream of mushroom soup
½ cup milk

" This will bring them in on a gallop - " Whoa "

In a large fry pan, cook the beef. Drain off most grease and add the onion, green chilies, olives, enchilada sauce, soup and milk. Bring to a low simmer . Allow to simmer for 3 to 5 minutes. Place a spoon full of sauce in each tortilla shell with a hand full of cheese. Roll up in a jelly roll fashion and lay in the fry pan with the sauce. Use up all the shells and let simmer to warm thru. Spoon sauce over the top of the shells and sprinkle cheese on top. Allow to sit for 2 or 3 minutes and serve with green salad and sour cream. For the extra hungry, add warm refried beans and rice.

Sometimes animals seem unconcerned when someone approaches closely, where as sometimes they disappear in a flash. Animals are sometimes startled by sudden movements and loud noises. Walk a soft path and talk in a soft voice for a better look at the animals of the wild. Remember they live there all the time and you are the intruder.

*** Fry Pan Baked Beans

8 strips of bacon chopped
1 green pepper sliced
1/3 cup brown sugar
1 can Coca-Cola

1 large onion sliced
1 tbsp. of mustard
½ cup catsup
2 cans kidney beans

In a large cast iron skillet, sauté the bacon. Add green peppers and onions, and stir till golden brown. Add all remaining ingredients and simmer for 20 to 25 minutes. This is a great side dish to serve with meals.

Please don't ask for Turtle soup. !!

*** Chicken Wings Coke Style

Take 20 to 25 chicken wings and place them in a warmed and oiled 12 inch Dutch Oven. Spray each layer with Vinegar water. Dump a can of Coke over the chicken and pour 3 cups of ketchup on top. Sprinkle 2 handfuls of brown sugar over the top of the chicken and cover. Place the Dutch over 10 coals and 15 on the top and replace as needed. , or in the Volcano with 12 briquettes. Follow previous campfire instructions or place in your oven at home. Wings take about 35 to 45 minutes. You'll smell them when they are ready. Try not to lift the lid.

The major environmental problem with trails are erosion, muddy stretches, and the developement of informal trails. Stay on the trails that are marked and encourage others to follow your lead. Only we the Public can help to preserve the wilderness for future generations.

*** Cowboy Sausage, Eggs & Biscuit Breakfast

Boil 8 eggs, peel and chop into pieces
Sauté and fry up 1-1/2 lbs. sausage or ham.
Add one medium chopped onion to the meat mixture.
Melt 3 tbsp. butter in a warmed 12 inch Dutch oven. Add 3 tbsp. flour,
1 tbsp. Log Cabin Seasoning or salt and pepper to taste. Stir and slowly
add 2-1/2 cups milk mixing & stirring well. Remove from heat when it begins
to thicken. Add 1 cup cheese, stir in meats and chopped boiled eggs. Add ½
cup sliced mushrooms. (optional). Return to fire and thicken. Serve over biscuits
If too thick, just add a little milk. Serve on toast, on hard bread, on French toast, Croissants or what
ever. Easy to store and reuse. Just add more milk to heat up.

*** Apple Toast

Peel, core and slice 5 or 6 apples. Put 2 Tbsps. Of butter in a 10 inch Dutch oven and melt down. Add
apples and sauté until transparent. Sprinkle them with 2 tbsp. powder sugar and 2 tbsp. water .Remove
from heat and put lid over coals. Quickly toast up 6 slices buttered bread. Put on plate and sprinkle on
a little powdered sugar. Spoon Apples on toast and serve.

When hiking, as with muddy stretches, it's better to cross low-angled snow banks than to skirt them and then create another trail. Wearing a pair of well fitted gaiters allows a hiker to walk briefly thru wet or muddy areas while remaining dry.

*** Outfitters Stuffed Green Beans

This recipe was an experiment created at **Outfitters Pack Station** in Idaho Falls , Idaho These guys are great friend and run a first class outdoor motel with a path. Stop and see them if your in your area, Dick cooks a great biscuit and Terri makes great coffee and muffins.

2 cups cut up cooked chicken
1 large can cream mushroom soup.
3 cans green beans   1 can sliced mushrooms and black olives
2 tbsp. Log Cabin Seasoning (salt & pepper)
2 cups French's French Fried onions or
1 Medium size onion chopped fine
1 pkg. chicken flavored stove top stuffing

" If you likE Em grEEN you'll love this oNE. !(!!!

Warm and lightly grease a 12 inch Dutch Oven. Spread a few onion slices in the bottom and lay the chicken over them. Sprinkle the bread crumbs and seasoning over the chicken. Next add drained green beans, seasoning, olives, mushrooms and remaining onion. Mix soup with milk and pour over the mixture. Sprinkle French Fried onions on top and cover. Bake with 10 Briquette under and 15 on top. Should take about 30 to 35 minutes. Remember to wait for the smell. In your Volcano, just put 12 briquettes and wait for the moisture and smell. Biscuits can be placed on top and baked for another 10 minutes to make a one pot meal.

People visit the back country because they both value and enjoy it., but "" We are loving our wilderness to death."" During a single night , over 1000 people camp in one valley in California's wilderness. Please Practice " No Trace –Low Impact—Camping. Love our wilderness enough to preserve it. Plan ahead—Know your area—Pack it in, Pack it out—and leave it clean for the next guy.

*** Crab Stuffed Chicken

6 boneless chicken breasts	1 lb. Crab meat
1 cup chopped celery	½ cup chopped onion
1 tsp. garlic	2 tbsp. Horse Radish
2 cups White Sauce(hold 1 cup for later)	2 tbsp. Log Cabin Seasoning
12 toothpicks	(Salt, and pepper,)

" You can please the experts with this one "Gourmet all the way"

Carefully cut breasts in half length wise. Spray Chicken with vinegar water, Mix all remaining ingredients together and place ½ cup mix on each breast. Fold 2nd half of breast over the top and secure with toothpicks. Sprinkle lightly with paprika and pour the remaining white sauce on top. Place 12 briquettes in Volcano, heat and oil Dutch oven place on coals and wait for the smell. 10 briquettes on bottom and 15 on top to cook with briquettes only. Should cook in about 50 minutes.

***White Sauce

4 tbsp. butter	3 tbsp. flour
1 tsp salt	½ tsp pepper
½ tsp onion salt	2 cups milk

Melt butter in sauce pan or 10 inch Dutch oven. Add flour, salt, pepper, onion and salt. Stir and add milk. Simmer over a low heat until thick. Set aside until needed. Sauce can be used on vegetables, meats and potatoes.

Vinegar mixture is 4 parts water and one part vinegar.

*** Breakfast of Champs Meat Loaf

1-1/2 lb. hamburger
1 medium onion chopped
½ tsp. salt—1/4 tsp. pepper
1 tbsp. Log Cabin seasoning
2-1/2 cups corn flakes, wheaties, cherrios or shredded wheat
2 eggs------------1 can cream of celery soup
¼ tsp. garlic salt or powder
1 can tomato sauce

This one will make a wrangler sing to his horses

Mix all ingredients together in a bowl except tomato sauce, or warm and lightly oil your 12 inch Dutch oven and mix in it. Form a ball in the center of the oven and cover with tomato sauce. Place on 12 briquettes in the Volcano or 10 underneath and 15 on top. Recipe should cook in about 50 minutes to an hour. You may have to replace briquettes as they burn down in the open air.

VARIATIONS;
Add potatoes, washed and quartered, with 2 cans of corn placed on top of potatoes.
Use chunky vegetable soup instead of celery
Use cream of mushroom instead of celery
Add 1 cup chopped fresh celery with mushroom soup

Always carry out what you take in while camping or hiking. In fact take as little in as possible and try to bring some out that others left. You will feel like your going the extra mile to help keep our wilderness clean and nice for others. Going the extra mile will help you feel as though the wilderness belongs to you too. It won't last forever unless we all care.

*** Get to Know Your Neighbor Soup

Just use your imagination, and you can invite a lot of friends and neighbors. Send or deliver the invitations to your neighbors with what to bring and be sure to have the date within 10 to 12 days. You'll have better attendance. Have a couple 12 inch deep Dutch ovens filled with broth, chicken or beef. Add the ingredients to the pots as they arrive. Kick back and visit as they arrive. Get to know each other and become better neighbors and friends. Helps to know who's who and who should be in your area. Great idea to start a neighborhood watch program.

Many Items can be added to these soups, just use your imagination. It works great.

Neighbor #1-----2 lbs. ground beef or chicken
Neighbor #2---- 1 can pinto beans
Neighbor #3-----1 can kidney beans
Neighbor #4-----1 can lima beans
Neighbor #5-----1 cup chopped celery
Neighbor #6-----1 large onion, chopped
Neighbor #7-----1 cup chopped mushrooms

You get the idea. Tomato sauce, cream soups, Potatoes, olives, green peppers, corn, peas, seasonings, ketchup, mustard and so on. Just make it fun. Don't forget the rolls and butter. Keep it simple and friends will come. You can furnish the plates, eating ware, drink and cooking surface. Dessert optional.

In 400 BC, Hippocrates used vinegar to treat his patients. He is known as the father of medicine. Vinegar was used as a dressing for healing wounds and infectious sores in biblical times.

*** Traditional Kentucky Burgoo — For a Big Party

One day I was sitting at a muffler shop while they were working on my car, and the girl next to me ask what I was working on. I explained about my cookbooks and she offered this recipe from her grandma in Kentucky.

20 lbs. turtle, venison, beef, pork or bird meat.----4 gallons cold water-----10 large bay leaves-----1/2 peck diced potatoes-----chop the following; 6 large onions-----3 stalks celery-----10 to 12 large carrots-----1 quart okra-----1 gallon corn-----4 green peppers-----1 tbsp. crushed hot peppers. Now add 2 tsp. Tabasco---4 tbsp. Worcestershire sauce-----1 cup apple cider vinegar-----salt and pepper to taste.

Trim the fats from the meat and place in a large black cast iron pot with the 4 gallons of water. Bring slowly to a boil and add the salt and pepper. Place the bay leaves in a sack tying the top closed and lower into soup. Put vinegar in soup mix and simmer while you prepare the vegetables. When meat is tender, remove from broth and cut into chunks. Add all the vegetables and return the meat to the pot. Simmer for 5 hours, replacing the water as needed. Keep heats as steady as possible. Salt and pepper as needed. About ½ hour before serving add the Tabasco sauce 1 tsp at a time tasting so as not to get too hot. Add Worcestershire and serve when ready over slices of bread or rolls. This recipe will feed about 50 to 60 people. Full simmer time will be around 6 hours.

Burgoo is a very old recipe cooked in Kentucky at barn buildings in order to feed all the people. This was also fixed during a Fox hunt to feed the hunters upon returning to the homestead. Most brought something to put in the pot, which accounts for all the different meats and vegetables. The sew was started and all would join together to eat after the hunt.   It's a great old recipe and story.

In the Autumn, Indians would grind the seeds of the Dock plant to use as their flour.

***Chili Noodle Dutch Oven Casserole

2 cans chili con carne   2/3 cup cocoa cola
1 cup chili sauce   ¼ tsp. pepper
8 ozs. Mozzarella cheese, grated
1 cup small curd cottage cheese
1/3 cup parmesan cheese
½ tsp. garlic powder   ¼ tsp oregano
4 cups wide egg noodles or,
4 ozs. of Lasagna noodles , cooked
1 cup cooked hamburger optional

In a warmed 12 inch lightly greased Dutch oven, combine Chili, cocoa-cola, chili sauce, spices and pepper. Heat thoroughly. Stir noodles into the mixture. Making little wells in the mix, drop cottage cheese into them. Spread cheese on top. Cover and return to the fire for 10 minutes or until the cheese is fully melted. Will serve about 10 to 12 people In your Volcano use 12 briquettes. 15 coals on top and 10 on the bottom. In a campfire push the coals back and pile around the sides of the pot.

Avoid damaging live trees and plants. We do not pound nails into trees to hang gear on, hack at them with hatchets or cut down live trees in the wilderness areas. Its O.K. to taste an edible plant, but please do not deplete the surrounding area.

***Campfire Beef Skillet Supper

In a 10 or 12 inch skillet, or a 12 inch Dutch oven bottom, which has been warmed and lightly greased, fry 2 lbs. of hamburger and one diced medium size onion. When fully cooked, drain off the excess grease and add 4 tbsp of your favorite steak sauce or Worcestershire sauce. Put in 2 pkgs. Of frozen green style green beans, 2 cans cream of celery soup and 2 cans mushroom pieces-drained. Stir enough to mix. Heat to a simmering boil, cover for 10 minutes. Sprinkle with garlic croutons or crushed Ritz crackers just before serving.

Wildlife; Respect for others in the outdoors also includes the wildlife. Keeping a safe distance from birds and animals will not force them to flee and you'll be able to enjoy them more. We can greatly effect the wildlife by destroying their habitat, so be very careful not to do so when you are hiking or camping. If you travel with a pet, never allow it to harass the wildlife. One of the neatest things is to observe the wildlife and have them come close enough to almost touch. I have actually had a deer nudge my hand because I was so still . There is nothing as exciting as watching a busy little squirrel or chip monk gather there food for storage and have them run across your lap as you sit quietly and watch. It's you outdoors, lets all protect it for future generations.

***Zucchini Casserole

4 medium zucchini
6 or 7 carrots or 1 lrg. pkg. Baby carrots
1 medium onion, peeled and cubed
1 cube butter or margarine
½ cup sour cream
1 can cream chicken soup
1 box stove top stuffing
1 cup crushed Ritz crackers

_This great recipe was shared with me by **Ed and Joyce Short of Sandy, Utah Good friends & great cooks.**

Good friends are worth more the Gold" Thank You God for the Gift of Friendship.

Boil carrots and sliced and peeled if desired zucchini in water for 15 minutes until tender. Drain off water. Put ½ cube butter in 10 or 12 inch Dutch oven with the onion and sauté When cooked, add soup, sour cream and uncooked stuffing and seasoning mix. Carefully stir in carrots and zucchini. In a small pot, melt remaining butter and pour over crushed crackers. Spread on top of mixture and cover. Cook for 30 minutes or until you can smell it. 12 briquettes in a Volcano, 10 briquettes on the bottom and 15 on top in the open air, and brush back the coals and surround the out side of Dutch oven with campfire coals. On a propane or gas fire, reduce the heat to low and put 12 or 14 briquettes on top. Just wait for the smell, it will tell you when it's done.

<u>Respect Private Property:</u> <u>Always be sure to get permission before crossing or entering private property. Give respect as well as ask for it.</u>

Page 39

***COWBOY POTATOES AND PEAS

8 medium potatoes
2 large onions
1 large package frozen peas
2 tbsp. log cabin seasoning (all purpose seasoning)
5 strips bacon
1 cup shredded cheese
1 tsp. salt
½ tsp. pepper

Cowboys can't be waistin time standin in line when it's time for chow!

In a 12 inch warmed and lightly oiled Dutch Oven, place the strips of bacon. Next place a layer of sliced onions and a layer of sliced or diced potatoes. Salt and pepper the layer and sprinkle 1/3 of the cheese. Now lightly sprinkle with the seasoning. Spray the layer lightly with the 4 to 1 vinegar solution. This is optional, but remember that tender things cook faster. Repeat layers of onions and potatoes and seasonings. Place on your Volcano on 12 briquettes and wait for the smell. At 1st smell, remove the lid and sprinkle on the remaining cheese and peas. Replace lid and let cook another 10 minutes. With regular cooking on briquettes, put 10 underneath and 12 on top, replace as needed to maintain heat. Approximately 50 to possibly 75 briquettes will be needed. Be sure to circle the briquettes under the outer rim of your Dutch Oven. In your oven at home, place your Dutch Oven on 350 degrees and wait for the smell. About 35 minutes, then remove lid and add remaining cheese and peas. Return to oven for 10 more minutes.

In order for us to leave the No Trace Camping, or Low Impact Camping ideas with all outdoor enthusiasts, we must practice them ourselves and be willing to tell others about them.

*** Stockman's Spicy Sauce

3 tsp. Onion powder
2 tsp. dry mustard
2 tsp. real salt
½ tsp. pepper
¼ tsp. Tabasco sauce
4 tbsp. Worcestershire sauce

¼ cup brown sugar
2 cups tomato sauce
2/3 cup vinegar
½ stick butter
a pinch of thyme

add more if you LiKE it Hot.

Great on Ribs & wings

Combine all ingredients, shake or beat well before using as a basting sauce. For dip or gravy sauce add 1 tbsp. tomato paste and ¼ cup tomato sauce to recipe and cook down to a thick consistency.

***Hitchin Post Barbecue Sauce

½ cup Sherry Wine
3 tbsp. onion powder
1-1/2 tsp. Worcestershire sauce
1 tsp. brown sugar
½ tsp. garlic
¼ cup vinegar

¼ cup salad oil
½ tsp. garlic
¼ tsp. salt
1 tbsp. dry mustard
1/2 tsp. pepper
1 can tomato paste

MakEs mE want to Dance

Combine all ingredients and shake or beat well. Can be used to baste or marinade meats.

The only true way to dry cast iron is to heat it on the fire and let the moisture evaporate.

Page 35

*** Cattle Creamy Coke Eggs

In a 10 inch Dutch Oven that has been warmed and oiled, melt 4 tbsp. butter or Margarine. Blend in 4 tbsp. flour, ¼ tsp. salt, and 1/8 tsp. pepper. Cook slow, stirring often to keep from burning. Mixture will become thick and bubbly. Remove from the heat and add 1-1/2 cups coke and 1-1/4 cups milk. Return to the heat and bring to a slow boil. Gently stir in 6 eggs that have been whipped together. Let mixture simmer until cooked. Serve over English muffins, toast, rice, French toast or biscuits. Good breakfast dish that's different.

A great Campfire is a good way to get close to your family and build lasting memories. Always build your fires in an established fire pit, or in a 50 gallon barrel that is off the ground. Being careful of Forest Fires is an important way to help Woodsy Owl and Smokey Bear teach your children a good camping lesson. Make back country cookin a priority for you and cook responsibly. Use stoves with legs, like Volcano's, Log Cabin Pot bellies, Camp Chef, Webber and Coleman. Practice " No Trace Camping " where ever you go. Strain your dish water So.'s not to leave food particles lying around. Pack groceries carefully and plan your menu's to save time and carry out garbage. Repack all tin foil items in zip lock bags to avoid leaving foil in the back country. As you know, tin foil never disintegrates & Tin cans take 200 years. Make sure your grocery list is back country friendly. Keep it simple and make it taste good. We only have so much camping area and we must learn to keep it in great condition and preserve it for future generations.

Lets Build a good Campfire

Page 36

BREADS AND VEGETABLES

***Breads and Vegetables cont.

As you already know, there are as many kinds of bread recipes as there are cakes. You can use baking soda, yeast, baking powder, eggs, fire ash and other things to raise your bread. The more you work the air into your bread dough, the lighter it will be. When Dutch Ovens came to be, it brought a new concept to baking bread and the taste is only enhanced with the seasoning and oils in the oven. Pioneers used " Pearlash or Saleratus to raise there bread and cakes. Today we call it Baking soda. They gathered it in creek beds along the Sweetwater river as they traveled thru Wyoming.. They added a little Cream of Tarter to blend in with the natural soda to soften the bitter taste. I hope to give you some different bread recipes and great tasting veggies dishes to help add to your Dutch Oven enjoyment.

The least liked of the bread recipes was called Hardtack. It was made from flour mixed with just water and flour. Sometimes a little salt was added, and baked a long time in a slow baked oven until hard. Some referred to it as pilot bread or sea biscuits. When hard rains came to the plains as they traveled, the pioneers were forced to eat hardtack dipped in cold coffee or water, because they could not build fires with wet chips or wood. The hardtack resembled a cracker shape. If you have never tried any, do so with your children and let them experience real pioneer food.

Before building a fire, consider the following factors; Surroundings, wind conditions, availability of the right wood, location and administrative restrictions. Low impact camp fires are built with only dead and downed wood. Never use green tree branches or chop down trees.

***Flour Tortillas

Mix together, 3 cups flour, 1 tsp. salt, 2 tsp. baking powder, and cut in 3 tbsp. shortening or lard. Add enough water to create a stiff dough. Make your dough into balls the size of a golf ball or larger if you prefer. Roll into circles, or mash flat with your hands. Cook on an ungreased cast iron griddle or the lid to your Dutch oven. There will be brown spots on each side. Don't over cook, and serve in place of bread or with Mexican food dishes. Great for Taco's and Enchiladas Sometimes I'll add a little Onion or Garlic powder to the dough for a great taste. Can be served with just butter and jam or syrup. Top with Chili, Hamburger, Cheese, Tomatoes, Onions, chopped Olives, Lettuce, Sour Cream and etc., makes a full meal. Great for camp trips and lite suppers.

***Crackling Corn Bread

"This is a fun Recipe"

Mix up a batch of Corn meal, add an extra ½ tsp. of salt and a cup full of crushed pig cracklings. (Sometimes called pig skins) . Pour into a warmed, greased 12 inch Dutch Oven. Place on 12 coals in your Volcano, or 10 on the bottom and 15 on top with just briquettes. Add more as needed. Bake at 350 in your own oven or in the Log Cabin stove use 12 on the bottom and 13 on top. This recipe dates back to the early 1800's and was used by my Grandma when she would render the Lard out of Pig fat. Cracklins are the crisp remains of the fat. In your Log Cabin Pot Belly, use 12 briquettes on the middle grill in a circle.

When camping, be sure to avoid places where impact is just beginning. Stay in designated camp spots. Most campsites can withstand a certain level of use. But all campsites can not regenerate themselves. Find a spot that can be used responsibly. Allow spots to regenerate for future use.

***Easy Cornmeal Tortillas

Combine 1 cup yellow cornmeal, ½ cup real salt, and ½ cup flour in a medium bowl. Stir in 1 egg and 2 cups water until smooth. Heat and lightly grease a small fry pan.. Spoon 3 to 4 Tbsps. batter into a hot pan. Turn and twist immediately to cover bottom of pan. Cook 30 seconds, then flip and cook other side. Do not over cook. Layer cooked tortillas with paper towels to keep from sticking. About 20.

***Mama Belle's Dinner Rolls *" This was mama's favorite + we love'd em "*

In a small bowl, dissolve 2 pkgs. of dry yeast in 1 cup warm water. In a large bowl or a 12 inch Dutch Oven Bottom, { warmed and oiled }, put 1 cup boiling water, 1 cup shortening, ¾ cup sugar and 1 tsp. of real salt. Stir a little until shortening is melted and sugar has dissolved. Add the yeast mixture and beat in 2 eggs.   Now add 2 cups of the flour, half white and half wheat if you wish, and mix till smooth. Add about 5 ½ to 6 more cups of flour until the dough forms a soft ball. Do not over knead. Place in a greased bowl and turn to coat with oil. This can be covered and refrigerated over night or let rise and cook as rolls, twist bread, fry bread or crescents. Pinch off a piece, roll into a rope and tie in a knot. Place in a Dutch oven or on a cookie sheet and cover. Let rise for 30 minutes and Bake at 350 degrees for 30 minutes In your Volcano it will bake on 12 briquettes for about 25 minutes. Over briquettes it will take in a 14 inch 12 on the bottom and 17 or 18 on top.

Twist bread will take 2 12 inch ovens, Rolls only 1. On a camp fire, remember to brush back the coals and place the oven on the ground. Pile coals about 1/3 the way up the oven and wait for your smell. These make great cinnamon rolls too. Should yield 2 to 2 ½ dz. Rolls. In your Log Cabin Pot Belly stove, 12 briquettes in a circle middle grill. On a camp chef, low bottom heat and 12 briquettes on top.

***Western Italian Cheese Loaf

In a mixing bowl dissolve1 dry yeast packet in 1 ¼ cups warm water. Add 2 tbsp. sugar, 1 ½ tsp. garlic salt, ¾ cup grated cheese, 1 tsp real salt and 2 cups flour. Beat until smooth and add just enough flour to make a soft dough. About 2 to 2 ½ cups more flour. Knead until smooth and elastic in appearance on a floured surface. Place in a warmed and greased 12" Dutch oven. Let rise until double in size. Punch down and divide into two loaves. Return to the greased Dutch Oven Cover and place 2 briquettes on the lid. (This will help the dough to rise faster.) After about 20 to 25 minutes look at the dough if double in size,-- place the oven on 10 briquettes, with 15 on top, bake until you can smell it. It will tell you when it's done by the smell. On charcoal only, 15 on top and 10 on the bottom. In the Log Cabin Pot Belly Stove, 12 briquettes in a circle. Diagonal slits can be made in the top of the bread before baking and sprinkled with garlic and grated cheese. Romano, Cheddar, Provolone, Swiss, Monterey jack or Etc. Baking time will be around 25 minutes to 30 minutes.

Did you know, that in the Early Days a full day was devoted to baking of Breads, Pies, & Cakes. Bread making was a real art. Brick ovens next to the hearth was built special for the lady of the house to use for her baking. A fire was built in the fire place and good hot coals were transferred up to the oven. When it was thought that the oven was the right temp., baking began. It sometimes took 2 hours to get the oven ready. Coals were removed and the oven swept clean. A little flour was thrown in and if it took a about 30 seconds to brown the flour, the cook knew it was ready. A long handled wood flat shovel was used to remove the hotbread or cakes.

This is an Italian Specialty

***Sloans S-nut Rolls

2 loaves of frozen bread dough {UN thawed}.
Mix together;
1 cup creamy small curd cottage cheese
1 egg
½ cup melted butter
1 cup brown sugar
1 cup nuts, optional.
1 tsp vanilla or maple syrup

Cream makes soup taste re---al good.

Roll dough out in a rectangle, both loaves, and spread ½ the mixture on the top of each dough. Roll the sides up and cut into ½ in thick rolls Warm and grease a 12 inch Dutch Oven, or 2 10 inch Dutch ovens. Take each roll and twist once into a S strip. Place in the ovens, and let rise till double in size. About 30 minutes in the Dutch oven with the lid on. Will take 1 to 1 ½ hrs on a cookie sheet. Bake on 12 briquettes in your Volcano, or 10 on the bottom and 15 on top in the open air. In your oven at home, 350 degrees for 25 to 30 minutes or until you get the smell. Should make about 2 dozen rolls.

In most households, a full day was devoted to baking breads, cakes , pies etc. to last a few days in order to give the cooks time to gather and dry other foods. Much can be said about the skill of baking bread. Combining the right ingredients, cooking at the right temperature and cooking for the right amount of time with no clocks, temperature gauge or timers required some skill. The ovens in most hearths were built into the wall of the fire place and heated by building a fire in it, scraping out the ashes and coals and placing the bread on a wood board inside.

Civil War Corn Bread
I'm not sure where this recipe came from but
it is supposed to be from Mississippi.

Mix ¾ cup flour, 1 ½ cup Corn meal, 2 tbsp. sugar, 1 tsp. baking powder and 1 tsp. Real Salt together in a mixing bowl or bucket. Fluffy or sift to combine well. Whip up the 2 eggs and 1 ½ cups milk{or substitute sprite or 7-up.} and add to the flour mix. Stir in the shortening, ¼ cup melted or use liquid margarine. Pour into a greased and warmed 10 inch Dutch oven or if you like thin slices, put in a 12 inch oven. Bake on 12 briquettes in your Volcano or Log Cabin Pot Belly Stove, 10 on the bottom and 12 on top in the outdoors or in the campfire push back the coals and set the oven on the ground. Pile coals about 1/3 of the way up the oven. In your oven bake at 350 and wait for the smell. Should be around 30 minutes. Add briquettes if needed in the open air.

Hoe Cakes
These were used extensively during the civil war

Try these just for fun"

1 tsp. salt and 4 cups cornmeal mixed together. Enough boiling water to make a stiff batter. Moisten your hands and flatten 1 tbsp. of batter into a paddy. Fry on a hot rock or small griddle over the fire. While hot, butter and add jam to eat. Better eaten while warm. Doesn't sound to appetizing, but when its all you have its not to hard to get down.

When packing your food and supplies, repackage everything in easy to dispose of containers. Such as; plastic zip lock bags and paper. This makes less to pack in and less to haul out. Most paper can be burned in small amounts and plastic can be melted down to almost nothing. Think ahead and it will save a lot on your behind.

***Zucchini Bread

Mix together well;
1 cup oil
1 ½ cups sugar
3 tsp. vanilla
1 tsp. Real salt
1 tsp. soda ------3 eggs
2 tsp. cinnamon----1 tsp. nutmeg
¼ tsp. baking powder
3 cups flour-----1 cup nuts /optional

Nuts are optional But I think they're Gre---at

Warm and grease a 12 inch Dutch oven. Bake on 350 degrees for 45 minutes in your oven at home,   12 briquettes in your Volcano, 15 on top and 10 on the bottom for briquettes only, and in a campfire be sure to bake low and slow. Brush back the coals and place Dutch oven on the ground. Put coals half way up the sides and turn every 10 minutes to rotate the side from the fire. Wait for the smell, it's a self timing oven. In the Log Cabin Pot Belly stove, 12 on the bottom in a ring.

Selecting a good campsite and proper fire pit placement, , are meaningless without a thorough cleanup. Plan ahead and don't be in a hurry to leave the campsite. Sometimes avoiding a morning campfire is a good thing. You can leave without any worry of hot coals being left behind. Always make sure your fire pit is cold, wet and dead out. When you burn, break or saw only the amount of wood you will use so as not to leave behind a big pile. Wood scattered around will be a lot easier to show No trace camping

***Sourdough Starter

1 pkg. dry yeast
2 cups warm water
2 cups flour

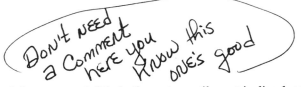

Don't need a comment here you know this one's good

Empty yeast into a warm mixing bowl {room temp.} Stir in the water until yeast is dissolved. Add flour and blend well. Cover top with a plastic bag and let stand at room temp. until bubbly and yellowish in color on top. {about 36 to 48 hours.} Store starter in a jar with a loose fitting lid in the refrigerator. Every time you use some of the starter, you must replenish it with 1 cup flour, 1/3 cup sugar and 1 cup milk. This can keep your starter going for years.

***SOURDOUGH BREAD

Dissolve 1 pkg. of dry yeast in ¼ cup warm water. Stir in 1 tsp. Sugar and let sit for 15 minutes. Mix in 1 egg, ¼ cup vegetable oil or bacon grease, ½ cup water, 1 tsp. Real salt and 1/3 cup sugar. Ad 1 cup sourdough starter, mix well and add 2 cups flour. Blend in well. Add remaining 1-1/2 cups of flour. Turn out on floured board, flour hands and knead 10 to 15 times. Add more flour if sticky. Oil the sides and bottom of 12 inch Dutch Oven. Put dough in the warmed and greasy Dutch Oven. Cover and let rise for 1 to ½ hour. Punch dough down and knead again. Shape into desired rolls or loaves and allow to rise again in the Dutch oven. When double in size, bake at 350 for 25 to 30 minutes. In your Volcano it takes 12 briquettes, on briquettes it's 10 bottom and 12 on top, replace as necessary.. Campfire instructions above, and in the Log Cabin Pot Belly stove, 12 briquettes on the middle grill in a circle on the bottom.

Build your fires in the most pronounced and safest preexisting fire ring in the camp site. Dismantle other fire rings in the area.   Try to leave your site as clean and attractive as you would like to find it on a return trip to the area.

***A Bit about Sourdough.

Years ago the chuckwagon cook was responsible for the sourdough batter . The container was usually a nine-gallon high wine keg. or crock. Into it went 4 or 5 quarts of flour, some salt and lukewarm water. If it was the 1st time to use the wooden keg, the first batch was dumped or used to chink the logs in a cabin. The keg was kept by the fire to be warm and allowed to ferment for 2 days. In the summer it was placed in the sun. Some added pieces of raw potato or molasses , pickle juice or apple vinegar might be used to hurry the process. The starter was minded carefully to keep the process going. When the process was finished, the camp cook was very well liked. He usually was treated royally. Especially if he was a good cook. His horses were well cared for and he always had a drink of whiskey if he wanted one. You always knew if his Sourdough and Dutch oven were out that you were in for a special treat. Sometimes the cook would sleep with the starter to keep it working in winter time.

***SOURDOUGH SECRETS

1. Avoid mixing to much, over mixing kills the gases needed for rising.
2. Sourdough requires slightly more heat and possibly longer cooking time.
3. Use lukewarm water. Never HOT or COLD.
4. Baking soda turns the batter yellow so use baking powder.
5. Batter should be at room temperature to use
6. Warm you pan or crock before attempting to make sour dough.
7. Using buttermilk as a liquid require more leavening so add baking powder.
8. Wheat flour won't raise as high as white but works faster.
9. Sourdough can be kept forever in your freezer and improve with age.
10. Never put anything but flour or water back in the starter pot.
11. If starter turns orange, throw it away.

Idaho Sports Outlet Crew Biscuits

Every year on the 3rd weekend of May, the crew in Pocatello, Idaho have a Dutch Oven Rendezvous. People come from all over to sample the food and learn about the Black pot cookin.. This is a recipe that the crew serves and shared with all who came. You'll never meet a greater bunch. Drop by just to visit and tell them Colleen sent you. The treatment will be royal and you can even get a big hug.

Mix 6 cups flour, 1 tsp. Real salt, 2 tsp. baking soda, 2 tsp. baking powder and 1 tsp. cream of tarter together in a bowl.   Rub in the softened 2 tbsp. of butter or margarine with your finger tips and add just enough milk to make a spongy dough. Mold into rolls or loaves as you prefer and let stand for ½ hour in a warmed , greased 12 inch Dutch oven. Place over 12 briquettes in your Volcano and wait for the smell. Or, put 10 on the bottom and 15 on top of your oven. Bake in your oven at home on 350 degrees. This will take approximately 20 to 30 minutes, or wait for the smell.

You can add a handful of currents or raisins for a variety. Brush the tops with butter or milk for a golden look or turn upside down on the lid to serve. These biscuits can be used as fry bread also.

Sports Outlet is on 655 E Lewis ST. Pocatello, Idaho   "Go Visit, you'll love em"

When putting out your fires, try to burn all the wood to ashes. Let the ash cool so's that you can run your fingers thru it. Crush the remaining charcoal and scatter the ash around widely. Scatter your unburned fire wood unless you are in a designated campground. Pick up burned food remnants and pack it out with your trash. Wilderness camping is a lot more demanding than campground overnighters. After a fire in the wilderness, camouflage the area and fill in any fire pits.

When gathering wood, be sure to use the deadwood in the area and collect wood from standing green trees.

A Happy Camper Layered Stew

This is a must do recipe, we experimented on a Dutch Oven class at a Happy Camper
Store in Twin Falls, in the Magic Valley Mall.
Donna Arrington owner Mgr.-great taster.

Donna's 1 pot meal.

2 lbs. Hamburger
7 med. Potatoes {washed and sliced}
1 large onion, sliced
1 large can chili
1 cup garlic spaghetti sauce
1 can peas
2 tbsp. Log Cabin Seasoning or Volcano all purpose
1 cup grated cheese, white, yellow or both

Put hamburger in the bottom of a warmed and oiled 12 inch deep Dutch Oven. Mash out to cover the entire bottom. Layer potatoes, onions, peas ½ sauce and ½ chili. Sprinkle seasoning and layer again until all veggies are used up. Mushrooms can be added, celery, squash, turnips or what ever you have. Italian sausage can be crumbled on top of mixture. Place on your Volcano with 12 briquettes or on your Log Cabin Pot Belly stove with 12 briquettes on the middle grill. With briquettes only, put 10 on the bottom and 15 or 16 on top. Add more as needed because cooking time will probably be about an hour and 15 minutes. The smell will tell you when it is done. In your oven at home, just turn it to 350 and wait for the smell. When it is done, remove the lid and sprinkle the cheese on top. Replace the lid, prepare your serving plates and cheese will be melted and stew ready to serve.

Page 47

***VEGGIES VEGGIES EVERY WHERE.

***Glazed Cheese Onions.

5 or 6 med. Onions
5 Tbsps. Butter
½ tsp. Real salt
½ tsp. bloke pepper
½ tsp. celery salt
½ cup dry sherry
2 tbsp. parmesan cheese

Peel and slice onions. Separate and set aside. In your Texsport cast iron wok, melt butter and add all ingred. Except sherry. Pour in onions and sauté until transparent. Add sherry and cook for 3 minutes. Sprinkle with parmesan and serve with any meat. Much better if served warm.

"want to share a mushroom"

***Flaming Rum Mushrooms

4 cups mushrooms washed off.
6 tbsp. butter
1 tsp. lemon juice
¼ tsp. Real salt.
½ tsp. pepper
3 Tbsps light rum, heated
½ cup heavy cream

Melt butter in your Texsport cast iron wok. Add lemon juice, Pepper and Real salt. Heat and add mushrooms, Sauté until warmed thru. Drain and add rum. Ignite the rum with a match. When fire is out, Stir in heavy cream and stir lightly. Serve as a vegetable dish or as sauce over any meat   Great with steaks of any kind.

AN UNCOVERED LEMON PEEL WILL ABSORB ODORS IN YOUR REFRIGERATOR BETTER THAN BAKING SODA.

***DOUBLE SQUASH CASSEROLE

In warmed and oiled Dutch oven, layer sliced zucchini or yellow squash. Slice 2 tomatoes and place on squash. Slice one onion and put on tomatoes. Salt and pepper the veggies and sprinkle on grated white cheese or cheese of your choice. Sprinkle ½ `tsp. tarragon. Repeat the layers and bake at 350 for about 35 to 40 minutes. Very good with any meat.

<u>SOME PEOPLE ARE LIKE POTATOES</u> " Worth Thinkin about "

Some people are bossy and like to tell everyone what to do, but of course they do not wish to soil their hands. They are called " Dick- Taters. "

Some people never seem to be motivated to participate. They are content to watch while others do. They are " Speck Taters "

Some people never do anything to help, but they are gifted st finding fault with the way others do things. They are called " Couch Taters ".

Some people are always looking for ways to cause problems. They look for other to agree with them. They are called " Aggie Taters "..

Then there are those that say they will but somehow never get around to doing anything. They are " Hezzie Taters."

Some people put up a front and act like they are someone they are not. They are "Emma Taters. "

Still there are those who live what they talk. They are always prepared to stop what they are doing to lend a hand. They bring sunshine into others lives. They are called "Sweet Taters".

<u>Lord help us to know what kind of Tators we are.</u>

***Cowtown Baked Stuffed Potatoes

Bake 6 large potatoes and let cool. Cut potatoes in half when cool. Try not to over bake the potatoes as they will go mushy. Carefully scoop out the inside of the potato and combine with 1 cup sour cream. Mix together well and add a packet of dry ranch dressing. Fill the potato skins with the mix and sprinkle the top with paprika and grated cheese. Warm your 12" Dutch oven and lightly oil. Place your filled potato skins in the oven, stacking if necessary. Bake in the Dutch oven for 15 minutes. You can add chili, cream soups or etc. to the potato meat.

***Camp fire Potatoes.

8 potatoes	5 onions
½ cup oil	2 lbs. bacon
seasonings Salt pepper garlic or what ever.	

Put the 2 lbs. of bacon in a warmed 12 " Dutch oven. Sauté until the bacon is almost done. Slice all potatoes and onions in the oven. Season as you go. Place lid on and put 12 briquettes in your Volcano. For briquettes use 10 on bottom and 15 on top. In your oven, place on 350 and wait for the smell. Recipe should take about 25 to 30 minutes.

***Country Glazed Carrots.

In a 12" Dutch oven, after warming and oiling lightly, place 2 lbs. carrots cut in slices. Melt 3 tbsps. Of butter and 1 cup of water with 2 tsp. of salt in the oven. Bring to a simmer and cook for 20 minutes with the lid on. Remove the lid and add 2 tbsp. brown sugar and ½ cup apricot jam. Cook over low heat until carrots are glazed. Takes about 5 minutes.

***Paprika   Potatoes and Butter

6 large potatoes, peeled, cooked and diced
½ cup butter or margarine
1 tsp. paprika
1 tbsp. Log Cabin seasoning or all purpose seasoning

Look who came to your Picnic

In a large cast iron skillet or bottom to a 12 inch Dutch oven, melt the butter.   Slowly sauté the potatoes until Golden Brown. Should take about 10 to 15 minutes. Sprinkle the seasoning and paprika over the top of the potatoes. Add salt and pepper if desired and serve. 6 to 10 servings.

***Mormon Baked Beans

Soak 2 cups beans and 6 cups water overnight, or simmer in a 10 inch Dutch oven with ½ cup apple cider vinegar for 1 hour. Add 1 chopped onion to the beans, with 1 ½ tsp. Real Salt and ½ tsp. pepper. Continue to simmer as you mix together, ¼ cup oil, ½ cup brown sugar, 3 tbsp. honey, ¼ tsp. dry mustard and ½ cup bacon bits. Pour over the beans and stir gently. Should cover the beans. Put lid on Dutch oven and simmer for about 1 hour. Serve with hot bread or corn bread for best results.

TRASH; Trash is the definition of the non food waste brought into the back country., usually from packaged products. The best bet is to carry out all trash. Most paper products are packaged in foil lined paper that will not burn. This product should be carried out along with glass, foil, plastic and cans.

***Campfire Quick Beans
Some people do not like to take canned foods into the back country, but for a dish this easy it's great

1 cup red kidney beans	1 cup whole kernel corn
1 ½ cup water	½ tsp. chili powder
2 cups canned tomatoes	½ cup maple syrup
1 med. Onion chopped	¼ tsp. dry mustard
1 cup chopped up bacon	1 tsp. Real Salt
½ tsp. pepper	½ cup apple vinegar

"Stack Em High their good Eatin"

Place beans, water and tomatoes in a pot with ½ cup apple cider vinegar. Simmer until tender unless using canned beans.   Add onion and bacon and simmer for 20 minutes. Add the remaining ingredients and simmer to blend the flavors for 25 minutes. This is a great tasting recipe and has excellent taste. You can write home about this one.

***Barbecue Salt

1 lb. Brown sugar	1 ½ tsp. cayenne pepper
1 cup Real Salt	¼ tsp. cinnamon
1 ½ oz. Paprika	1 tbsp. garlic powder
2 tbsp. black pepper	

Add a little onion powder too -

You can't Beat this one on a steak

Mix all ingredients together and place in a sealed container and keep refrigerated.
Rub into the meat before you barbecue,

G.W. GORDON 'S VEGGIES

From time to time, I cook at Iron Blossom Condo's at Snowbird Ski resort in Utah. I met a fellow in summer of 1998 that gave me this delicious vegetable recipe.

10 fist or smaller new red potatoes
2 cups cauliflower
1 lg. Onion chopped
2 cups carrots
1 cup celery
¼ cup oil
2 envelopes beefy onion soup mix.

" Good friends are everywhere you have to be a friend to have a friend "

Quarter the new potatoes, and place all veggies in the 12 inch Dutch oven that has been warmed and lightly oiled. Stir in oil, and prepared soup mix. Simmer for 25 minutes on the coals, and add baby peas, broccoli, and corn on the cob if desired. This is a great recipe for veggies. Return to heat for another 10 to 15 minutes, and serve. A Can of cream mushroom soup can be added to this as you put in the peas, to create a gravy consistency. Great for camping, with a steak over the campfire or fish.

OPTIMISM; A cheerful frame of mind that enables a tea kettle to sing though in hot water up to its nose.

Try crushing 5 qts. Of popped corn and putting it thru your blender and using in place of rice to make Rice Pudding. Its very good. Unsalted of course.

CAJUN MUSHROOMS

When you meet the crew at Ace hardware and sports in Pocatello, Idaho, your gona know some of the finest people the USA has to offer. Emma Curtis and crew go all out to make your shopping or visit trip to their store an experience to remember. Just try it, you'll like it.

3 cups quartered mushrooms
½ c. chopped red peppers
3 tbsp. butter
1 tbsp. chopped garlic
1 tbsp. Tabasco sauce or less
3 cups whipping cream

1 cup crab meat
½ c. chopped green onions
1 tbsp. thyme
1 tbsp. Worcestershire sauce
½ tsp. Real salt
2 tbsp. chopped parsley

"Share these with a friend"

Warm and oil a 10 inch Dutch oven. Sauté the mushrooms in 1 tbsp. butter. Remove from oven and set aside. Now sauté the peppers, onions, thyme and garlic in the remaining butter until slightly cooked, add remaining ingredients and simmer for about 5 minutes or until the cream is partially reduced. Add salt and mushrooms and continue until the cream mixture begins to thicken and bubble. Sprinkle the chopped parsley over the top. Serve with bread sticks.

***Emma's Garlic Rolls;** Take Rhodes frozen rolls and allow to unthaw. Heat and oil a 12 inch D.O. Melt ½ cup butter and 4 finely chopped garlic. Roll each roll in the garlic butter to coat, and arrange the rolls in the oven. About 15 to 20 rolls. Place lid on top and allow to rise for 25 to 30 minutes. When rolls are filling the oven about 2/3 full bake over hot coals-- More on top and less on the bottom. 15 top, and 10 bottom. 12 coals in your Volcano and Log Cabin Dutch oven cook stove. 350 degrees in your oven at home and wait for the smell These are to die for. Sprinkle with Parmesan cheese to serve. About 35 to 40 minutes.

"Go for This"

Page 54

***Basil Mushrooms and Peas

Heat and lightly oil a 12 inch Dutch oven. Put 2 10 oz. Pkg.'s of frozen peas in and cook according to the instructions. Do not drain. Add 2 6. Oz cans of sliced or mushroom pieces drained. Put 1 tsp. lemon juice, ½ tsp. crushed basil , ½ tsp. Real salt and ¼ tsp pepper over the mixture. Cover and warm thru. About 20 minutes... Cut recipe in half for a 10 inch. In a volcano use 10 briquette, on the Log Cabin Pot Belly use 10 - 12 briquettes, With Briquettes only, use 10 on the bottom and 13 on top. Put a can of cream of Mushroom soup on top for a variety.

*** Ginger Sweet Potatoes and Carrots

There Just Great

In Spokane Washington there is a very special Family that has captured my heart. They befriended me at a Big Horn Elk show, held at the fair grounds. Mike, Renata, LIV and Jessica, there family, just like my second family. We've rode together, hauled rocks together, built fence , gathered branches, shared the birth of a beautiful baby. Can't ask for more than that. We have a mutual friend named Bob that's pretty special too. That Renata can cook real god, so here is one of her great recipes.

Peel and dice 4 sweet potatoes, and 8 large carrots. Warm a 10 inch or 12 inch Dutch oven and lightly oil it. Place sweet potatoes and carrots inside with 1 cube of butter. Lightly sprinkle on some ginger seasoning and ½ cup honey. Bake for 35 minutes or until you can smell it. 12 briquettes in your Volcano, 8 on the bottom and 13 on top with a 10 inch and briquettes only.

***Fried Onion Slices

In a 10 or 12 inch fry pan or Dutch oven bottom, heat ¼ cup Italian dressing, 1/8 cup water and ½ tsp. Real salt. Place sliced onions in the sauce and simmer. Turn the onions over and sprinkle with parsley, parmesan cheese, and paprika. Garlic can be added if desired, Cover and simmer for 2 to 3 minutes. Serve with steak, chicken, hamburger veggies or what ever. Great garnish.

*** Saucy Orange Beets

In an 8 inch Dutch oven, blend 2 tsp. cornstarch, 2 tsp. sugar, and a ¼ tsp. Real Salt. Stir in ½ cup cranberry juice cocktail. Stir over heat in your Volcano junior or on a stove. Heat till thickened. Add one can diced or sliced beets, drained. Fresh sliced beets can also be used.   Add ¼ tsp. grated orange peel., simmer uncovered for 10 minutes. About 4 servings.

*** Oregano Cabbage

" You won't know how good they are unless you try them "

In a 10 inch Dutch oven, combine ½ cup water, 2 crushed bouillon cubes, any kind, and ¼ tsp. oregano. Simmer while you shred 3 cups cabbage, and 1 cup carrots. Thinly slice 1 medium onion. Add veggies to the bouillon mix, cover and cook for about 15 to 20 minutes. Drain and serve.

In many wildland areas, water is a limited resource. Yet water is in demand for a variety of competing uses; it is necessary for plants and animals, and its a focal point of most campsite activities. Life around usually suffers when the quality of water is harmed. Do your part to help keep it clean.

***Stuffed Spaghetti Squash

1 medium spaghetti squash, cut in half and cleaned
¼ lb. hamburger
1 small onion chopped fine
½ green pepper finely chopped
½ cup sliced mushrooms
½ tsp. basil
½ tsp. oregano
1 tbsp. log cabin seasoning or,
¼ tsp. Real salt,
1/8 tsp. pepper
1 can stewed tomatoes
1 tsp. garlic powder

Mix all ingredients together and fill the squash. Bake in a 12 inch warmed and oiled Dutch oven. Bake for 35 minutes or until you can smell it. Sprinkle the tops with white cheese and return to the fire for 5 more minutes to melt the cheese. Cut squash in half, serves 4 people. !2 briquettes in your Volcano, and 25 briquettes if your cooking with just briquettes. 10 on the bottom, 15 on top. In your oven, 350 degrees.

Camping close to water is probably more appealing in desert camping. But unless you are along a major river or in an area where water is extremely abundant, you should avoid it.
Camping away from the water source will lessen the chance to have a problem with animals or others using the water source.

***Peppered Potato Slices

8 potatoes, scrubbed and sliced
1 lb. Bacon, chopped
2 cups sliced mushrooms
2 onions, chopped
2 green peppers chopped
1 cup mixed white and yellow cheese.

"Good for a side dish & very mouth waterin"

Sauté bacon in a 12 inch Dutch oven that has been warmed and oiled. Add onions, green peppers and mushrooms. Sauté 3 to 5 minutes and add potato slices. Stir to combine and place on 10 briquettes on the bottom and 15 on top. !2 briquettes in your Volcano or 350 in your oven at home. Cook for 35 minutes or until you can smell it, and remove lid to sprinkle the cheese on top. Replace the lid for 3 to 5 minutes to allow the cheese to melt.

*** One Pot Bean Dinner

Put 1 lb. Hamburger, ½ cup cooked bacon, 1 chopped onion, 1 can kidney beans , 1 cup catsup, 1 can butter beans, ¼ cup brown sugar, 3 tbsp. apple cider vinegar, 1 tsp. Real salt, ¼ tsp. pepper, ½ cup chopped green pepper, 1 tsp. liquid smoke, 2 tbsp. Worcestershire sauce, 2 large cans pork and beans in a 12 inch Dutch oven. Place over 12 coals in your Volcano, 10 on the bottom and 15 on top for briquettes only. 350 in your oven at home. Cook for 1 ½ hours serve with hot rolls.

Shallow catholes are much more appropriate in the dessert than surface defecation. They should be located far from water and campsites or trails. This will keep visual contact to a minimum. The ashes from your fire will act as a yeast dissolving the waste. It takes over 2 years for human waste to biodegrade. When camping in the back countries, try to keep your party to maximum of 10.

***Baked Onions Ala.-Dutch

6 or 7 medium size onions
1/3 cup butter or margarine
1 tsp Real salt
½ tsp. black pepper
¼ tsp Red pepper
1 tsp each garlic and onion salt
½ cup bread or cracker crumbs
3 eggs beaten well

my mom's the Best Cook Ever-

Good Appetizer

Add all ingredients to the well beaten eggs, except the onions. Wash and peel onions. Quarter onions 2/3 rds thru and open slightly. Place in a 12 inch warmed and oiled Dutch oven. Pour some of the mixture in each oven and cover. Bake for 15 to 20 minutes on 12 Briquettes in your Volcano and 10 on the bottom and 15 on top if cookin with charcoal only. In your Log Cabin Stove, place 10 on the bottom and 10 on top. You'll really enjoy these as a snack or too go along with a nice dinner. These can also be done in tin foil in a camp fire. You can add a variety of spices to change or enhance the recipe. It's a lot of fun to experiment at this also

There is a warmth and fellowship of high spirits when family's and friends go camping. Learn to check for permits and wood availability before you leave for your camp spot to keep from causing stress when you get there.

***Cubed Spicy Potatoes

In a 10 or 12 inch warmed and oiled Dutch Oven, place 8 chopped up pieces of bacon and Sauté until crispy. Add 7 medium potatoes that have been washed and diced in small pieces. Add 4 chopped up green onions, ½ cup beef broth, ¼ cup apple cider vinegar, ½ tsp. Oregano, ½ tsp. garlic, ¼ tsp. thyme, ¼ tsp. pepper and ¼ tsp sugar. Stir the potato mixture to coat lightly and bake on 12 coals in your Volcano. Using briquettes only, 10 on the bottom in a circle and 15 on the top. Potatoes will cook in about 35 minutes. This is a great potato dish to serve with your favorite meat dish. Chunks of left-over steak or chicken can be added to the potato dish for a complete supper or lunch. When potatoes are done, biscuits can be cooked on top of the dish for a one pot meal.

Be prepared with some gams when you are going camping with a family or friends. Relays are usually fun for all ages. Contests for calling Husbands, wives, members of the family or hogs can add excitement too. People like to throw things like rolling pins, cow pies, paper plates, rocks, tin cans, or pop balloons. Use your imagination, but make your cap-out a fun time to remember. Leave them wanting to go again.

Use These

***Excuses for your cook-out.
1. But I followed the recipe..........2. What taste ?? I'm sure that was sugar..........3. It's an old old recipe and some of the ingredients came across the plains.............4. That black stuff is part of the seasoning from the black pot........5. I'm still trying to perfect this recipe.......6. It just doesn't look like the picture..............7. Of course I use soap, how else can you clean your pot.......8. I thought you liked your food well done..........9. I always cook my TV dinners in a Dutch oven..........
10. Just consider the ashes as part of the trace minerals your body needs.

Desserts and Miscellaneous;

Easy Cobbler

1 can pie filling fruit
1 cake mix
1 can pop

       This is without a doubt the easiest dessert to fix when camping or entertaining. Warm and oil your 10 or 12 inch Dutch Oven. Place a can of fruit in the bottom and a cake mix over the top. Drizzle a can of pop over the top and bake. If there is a lot of juice, like peaches, drain part of the juice and save for later to drink. Here are some combinations to work with.

1. Cherries---Chocolate cake mix and coke
2. Cherries   Cherry cake mix and coke.
3. Apples-----Spice cake mix and Rootbeer
4. Cranberries---Butter cake mix and cream soda.
5. Fruit cocktail---White cake mix and 7-up.
6. Blueberries---White cake mix and cream soda.

Everybody's favorite

Let your conscience be your guide, there are a lot of combinations that are great. In the Scout cobbler contests. I've sampled everything from Jerky to gummy bears in their cobbler.
Crumbled up cookies and stale donuts make a unique topping. Don't forget the whip cream or the ice cream if it's available.

***Dutch Oven Sponge Candy

1 cup sugar
1 cup dark corn syrup
1 Tbsp. apple cider vinegar
1 Tbsp. baking soda

This is a good one.

In a 10 inch warmed and oiled Dutch Oven, heat sugar, corn syrup and vinegar to boiling. Stir until sugar is dissolved. Boil until candy thermometer reaches 300 degrees with out stirring. Another way to check it is to drop a small amount into cold water. If it separates into threads that are hard and brittle, remove from heat and stir in baking soda quickly and thoroughly. Pour mixture into 9x13 pan. Let it cool and break into pieces. Makes about 1 lb. Very good and can be flavored if you wish.

*** No Bake Rum Balls

In a bowl or 12 inch cold Dutch oven, mix 2 ½ cup crushed Vanilla wafer crumbs, 1 cup powdered sugar and 2 Tbsps. Unsweetened cocoa. Mix well, add 1 cup chopped pecans, ½ cup light corn syrup and ¼ cup white rum. Stir until well blended. Shape into balls and let stand 1 hour. This will allow the flavors to mix. Roll balls in powdered sugar and press a pecan into each ball. Store the balls in a tightly covered container for 3 days. These balls can be stored up to 1 ½ months. Makes about 5 dozen .

Careful meal planning for the back packer and camper, can result in little or no carry out trash.

***Dandelion Jelly

1 qt. Dandelion blossoms
2 qts. Water
1 1.75 oz. Pkg. pectin

5 ½ cups sugar
2 Tbsp. orange extract

Place blossoms in a 10 inch Dutch oven with the water, bring to a boil and simmer for 4 or 5 minutes.. Strain thru a sieve or cheese cloth. This should leave about 3 cups of water. Return liquid to Dutch, add pectin and boil, stirring constantly. Stir in sugar and simmer for 5 minutes. Add orange extract and simmer for 1 minute. Skim off the foam and pour jelly into sterilized jars. Process in boiling water bath for 5 minutes with lids on.

THIS IS A GREAT TASTING JELLY.

Try these with your kids " Lots of fun "

*** Fried Dandelion Blossoms

Pick yellow blossoms and thoroughly clean. Rinse in water with a little cider vinegar added and pat dry. In a bowl, put one egg and beat well. Add ¼ tsp. salt. Dip blossoms into egg mix and fry in a medium hot skillet that 4 tbsp of butter has been melted. Fry until golden brown and eat while hot. They get tough as they cool down.

All dish washing in the out of doors, should be done away from water sources. Soap is unnecessary for most dish washing jobs. A small amount of cider vinegar in the water is a disinfectant.

*** Dutch Oven Apple Pie

Line the bottom of a 12 inch warmed and oiled Dutch oven, press out flat, enough pie crust to cover the bottom of the pot and 2 or 3 inches up the side. Combine 6 cups of grated apples, with 1 cup sugar, 1 tsp. cinnamon, ¼ tsp. nutmeg, ¼ tsp. cloves, and ¼ cup warm water with 2 heaping Tbsp. of corn starch mixed in. Combine with apple mixture and place in oven. Place another pie crust on top, and brush with milk or beaten egg white. Bake in your volcano on 10 briquettes for 35 minutes and then transfer all the heat to the top to brown. 10 min. With briquettes only, put 15 0n top, 10 on the bottom and add as needed to maintain heat temperature. In your oven 350 and wait for the smell. Sprinkle top crust with cinnamon, nutmeg and sugar for a great taste. About 35/45 minutes.

*** Cattle Drive Fritters

2 cups flour	2 eggs well beaten
1 T. baking powder	1 cup milk
½ tsp. salt	2 ½ cups apples chopped fine
4 T. sugar	½ tsp. each cinnamon and nutmeg

" Cowboys run real hard for these "

Put all dry ingredients in a bowl and add milk and eggs that have been beat together. Refrigerate the batter for 2 hours or set in your cooler. Add the apples and drop by spoonful into 3 or 4 inches of hot oil. Fry for 3 to 5 minutes and roll in sugar and cinnamon mix or powdered sugar and cinnamon mix. This is a great treat and can be done in a 10 inch .Dutch oven. A cast iron wok also works very nice and **Texsport** has a great one.

Package your foods in zip lock bags to go camping, and you will cut down on the trash you have to carry out.

*** Vanilla Sauce

1 cup sugar--------------1 tbsp. flour---------------1/4 tsp. salt----------1 cup boiling water----------1 tbsp. butter------
----------1 tsp. vanilla.
 Blend the sugar flour and salt. Add to boiling water and stir until smooth. Simmer for about 3 minutes
and add the butter and vanilla. Serve over puddings.

*** Chocolate sauce

Chocolate sauce can be made by adding 2 squares of chocolate to this recipe

Good for lots of things

*** Lemon Sauce
Lemon sauce can be made by omitting the vanilla from this recipe and adding 3 Tbsp. lemon juice or extract and 2
Tbsp. grated lemon rind. Use orange juice and rind for orange sauce.

*** Caramel Sauce
2/3 cup corn syrup------1 ¼ cup brown sugar------4 Tbsp. butter-------3/4 cup evaporated milk.
 Cook all together in a 8 inch Dutch oven for 15 to 20 minutes over low heat or on 3 briquettes
in your Volcano. Beat for a few minutes with your hand mixer and add nuts if desired.
These are great sauces for puddings, cakes, dumplings or fruit.

*** Utah Pound Cake

¾ cup butter-------1/1/2 cups sugar-------3 eggs-------1 tsp. vanilla-------1/4 tsp almond or lemon extract-----1/2 tsp. salt--------3/4 cup milk-------1/2 tsp. baking powder-------2 1/3 cups flour.

Warm and oil a 10 or 12 inch Dutch oven. Beat butter and sugar until fluffy. Add eggs and flavorings mix well. Blend dry ingredients and milk into the mixture. Mix well and pour into Dutch Oven. Bake for 45 minutes or until you get the smell. Top will spring back when touched if done. This is a great cake to serve with any of the sauces.

*** Lincoln and Lee Pudding

1 cup brown sugar-----------1/4 cup butter------------2 cups water
½ tsp vanilla--------------1 cup flour---------1/3 tsp. salt
1 tsp. baking powder-------1/2 c sugar-----------1 cup milk-----
1 cup nuts------------1/2 cup raisins

In Boise, Idaho there is a couple of great Dutch oven Cooks. **Mel and Jan Eggleson.** They are the proud owners of *Kampers Kettle.* It's a unique little store with a lot Visit them on the web too.
Http:www.rmc.net/kampers

Bring to a boil, the brown sugar, butter, water and vanilla. Mix together flour , salt, baking powder and white sugar. Mix to thick batter with the milk, add nuts and raisins. Drop by spoonsful in boiling mix and then bake in moderate oven for 20 minutes. 10 briquettes in your volcano, with a 10 inch oven, and 8 on the bottom and 13 on top with briquettes only. On your stove, just simmer on a slow low heat. These can be served with whipped cream, ice cream or on of the sauces on the sauce page 65.
You'll love these and so will your guests.

*** Penrose Fudge Cake

1 cup soft butter-------------------2 cups sugar
1 cup flour------------------------4 tbsp. cocoa
4 eggs well beaten----------------2 tsp. vanilla
1 cup chopped nuts

This one's Scrumpteous

Add sugar to well beaten eggs. Sift in cocoa and flour. Work the butter in slowly and add the nuts and vanilla. Pour into a warmed and greased 10 inch Dutch oven. Bake on a low and slow heat for 50 minutes or until you can smell it. In your Volcano use 8 Briquettes, for briquettes only, 7 on the bottom and 11 on top. In your oven, 325 degrees. In your Log Cabin Dutch oven stove, 8 bottom and 6 on top.

*** Rum Sauce Delicious

2 cups powdered sugar----------1 cube, (½ cup) Butter
1 tsp. vanilla ------------------2 tbsp. rum.

You can use Koluaha - or Irish Cream too.

Cream butter and sugar together. Add vanilla and rum and mix well together. This is a great sauce for carrot pudding.

The primary consideration when washing yourself or your clothes is to avoid contamination of water supplies. Soap, even biodegradable, breaks down very slowly in cool mountain water. It is best to minimize its use and not allow it to enter lakes and streams at all.

*** Fresh Country Peach Cobbler

Filling;

1 c. sugar
2 eggs beaten
2 tbsp. cornstarch
½ tsp. nutmeg
4 c. fruit

Cobbler Crust;

4 tbsp. sugar------3 tbsp butter
1 ½ tsp. baking powder
½ tsp. salt   2/3 c. milk
1 c. flour

"Good for the Soul"

Warm and oil a 12 inch Dutch oven. In a large bowl mix all the filling ingredients except the fruit. Set aside, mix all cobbler ingredients together except milk and butter. Now mix in milk and butter, cutting them into the crust mix until ball forms. Now mix fruit into filling mix and pour into Dutch Oven. Crumble or spoon the crust mix over the filling. Sprinkle the top lightly with sugar and cinnamon. Bake on 12 briquettes in your Volcano, 10 on the bottom and 15 on top with briquettes only and in your oven, bake at 374 for 35 to 40 minutes. In your Log Cabin Dutch oven stove, 10 on the bottom and 13 on top.

Grandma would be so proud. A Dutch oven is the best way to cook a cobbler, the heat is real even and you can put brown sugar on the bottom for an extra crust.

*** Peach Cobbler

Melt ½ cup butter in a 10 inch warm Dutch oven. Combine 1 c. flour, 2 tsp. baking powder and 1 C of the sugar and ¾ c. milk. with the butter. Arrange sliced peaches over the mix. Sprinkle the ½ cup sugar over the peaches with a sprinkle of cinnamon and nutmeg. Drizzle ½ cup water over the peaches and bake at 350 degrees in your oven or 12 briquettes in your Volcano. 10 on the bottom and 15 on
top with briquettes only and 12 0n the bottom in your Log Cabin Dutch oven stove and 8 on
top. Bake about 45 minutes, the smell will tell you when it is done.

*** Steamed Carrot Pudding

Fine idea to triple this recipe or even more and give as Christmas gifts. This recipe will only keep for 30 days in the refrigerator.

1 c. raw carrots	1 c. sugar
1 c raw potatoes	1 tsp. each salt, soda, nutmeg,
1 c. flour	allspice and cinnamon
½ c. melted shortening	1 c. raisins
1 c. chopped nuts	

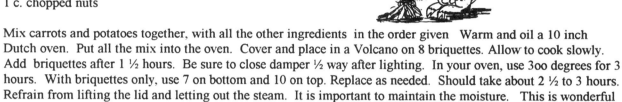

I mean everybody likes these

Mix carrots and potatoes together, with all the other ingredients in the order given   Warm and oil a 10 inch Dutch oven. Put all the mix into the oven. Cover and place in a Volcano on 8 briquettes. Allow to cook slowly. Add briquettes after 1 ½ hours. Be sure to close damper ½ way after lighting. In your oven, use 3oo degrees for 3 hours. With briquettes only, use 7 on bottom and 10 on top. Replace as needed. Should take about 2 ½ to 3 hours. Refrain from lifting the lid and letting out the steam. It is important to maintain the moisture.   This is wonderful with Rum Sauce or hard vanilla sauce or lemon sauce. Whipped cream or Ice Cream works well also.

When traveling where black bears or grizzly bears are present, camp organization and cleanliness take on a whole new meaning. The primary concern is safety, both for the bear and traveler. Personal safety is the first priority, a bear can be a very dangerous animal if provoked or habituated to humans. Potential for personal injury does exist and precautions should be taken. The bears live their, we are the visitors.

*** Cereal Caramel Cute puffs.

Try this ONE

In a 10 inch Dutch oven, melt 1 lb., 4 cubes, with 6 tbsp. water 2 cups sugar and 2 tbsp. light karo. Bring to a boil but do not stir after it starts to boil. Just as it begins to turn brown, Pour over 3 to 4 quarts of cereal. Such as – Cheerios, Shredded wheat squares (small), Frosted flakes, Rice Crispies, Fruit loops, Corn Pops and etc. This is a fun recipe when camping and a good snack. Almost any cereal can be used and you can do it in a deep 14 inch oven to coat .. Be careful not to get burned, as the syrup will be definitely hot.

*** Buttermilk Donuts for Brigham

This recipe supposedly came from Emily Dow Partridge Young, a wife of Brigham Young.

you don't have to wait for christmas

"Kids LOVE EM"

2 c. buttermilk	1 tsp. baking powder
2 eggs beaten	2 tsp. Real Salt
5 c. flour	1 tsp. nutmeg
1 c. sugar	11/4 cup melted butter or oil"
2 tsp. baking soda	

Combine the buttermilk, eggs and sugar. Mix well. Add all dry ingredients and melted butter. Mix to dough and roll out ¼ inch thick.. Cut into desire shapes or use a donut cutter. Fry in hot oil heated in a Dutch oven to 350 /375 degrees until golden brown. Drain on a paper towel, and sprinkle with sugar and cinnamon. Can also be frosted with any flavor frosting.

When Backcountry Horsemen approach you on the trail, please be courteous and step off to the down side of the trail if possible. This will allow the horses to pass without much impact to the terrain. Try to find a good spot to pass each other if possible.

*** Master Mix for Baking

If you mix up a big batch of this for camping, it will make everything you need. Rolls. Biscuits, pancakes, cookie, cobbler crust and etc.

9 c. sifted all purpose flour   4 tsp. Real salt

1/3 cup baking powder   ¼ c. sugar

1 tsp. cream of tarter   1 cup dry milk

Keep this one handy

Using a large bowl, mix all the ingredients together. Fluff them with a wire whip or sift to be sure they are combined well. Store in a gallon jug or large plastic container with a lid.

Pancakes with master mix

3 cups master mix, combined with 1 ½ cups water , ¼ cup oil and 2 eggs or 2 tbsp. powdered eggs. Mix well, makes about 16 pancakes. Cut in half or less to shorten the recipe. Remember that above 6500 feet elevation, you can use a carbonated drink such as 7-up or cream soda to help the leavening agents work harder. Any carbonated water will work.

Biscuits with the master mix

3 ¼ cups master mix with 2/3 cup liquid. Can be any pop that is carbonated. Stir with a fork just enough to coat the flour and drop by spoonful into a warmed and oiled Dutch Oven. 10 minutes baking time on 425 at home in your oven, 12 briquettes in the Volcano, 10 on the bottom and 15 on top for briquettes only.

*** Beer Bread

3 cups master mix in a bowl mixed with 3 tbsp. sugar. Dump in 1 can of room temperature beer and mix well.
Pour into a 10 or 12 inch Dutch oven and bake over 12 coals in your Volcano, 350 degrees in your oven at home,
10 coals on the bottom and 15 on top for a 12 inch with briquettes only. In you Log Cabin stove, 10 on the bottom
and 10 on top. This should take about 50 minutes. The smell will tell you when its done.

*** Dutch oven Apple Crisp

my Kids love it

Substitute canned Apples pie filling if you wish

Warm and oil a 12 inch Dutch oven Place 4 cups of freshly sliced apples in the pot and sprinkle ½ cup brown
sugar and 2 tsp. apple pie spice over the top. Mix together 2 cups oatmeal, ½ cup brown sugar, ½ cup white
sugar, 1 tsp. cinnamon, ½ cup melted butter and 1 tbsp. flour. Sprinkle over the top of the apples. In your
Volcano, put 12 briquettes on the bottom and wait for the smell. Should take about 20 to 25 minutes. With
briquettes only, 10 on the bottom and 15 on top. In your Log Cabin Stove, use 12 on the bottom and 2/3 of the way
thru the cook time transfer all the heat to the top.

*** Dutch Oven Cracker Jacks

Your gona love it Baby !!

2 cups sugar----------------------1 cup molasses --------------------2 Tbsp. apple cider vinegar
              Boil above ingredients in a 10 inch Dutch oven until they reach the crack stage when
dropped in cold water. Take from the fire and add ½ tsp. soda. Beat briskly with a wire whip. Pour
over 2 qts. popped corn and mixed nuts.

Let me say it again, " ALWAYS RESPECT PRIVATE PROPERTY ".

THERE ARE SO MANY BEAN AND SOUP RECIPES, THAT I THOUGHT MISC.. IS A GOOD PLACE TO PUT THEM.

A few years a go I met a very nice guy from Chicago named John Kulovits. He shared with me a recipe he makes for his family quite often. So---I thought I would share it with you.

Smoked Sausage Barley Stew

SERVE with
Garlic CHEESE Rolls
it's great

16 oz of smoked sausage cut into pieces
1 medium onion chopped
2 ½ cups beef broth
4 sliced carrots
½ head cabbage cut into pieces
4 medium red potatoes cut into pieces
¼ cup quick barley
1 can stewed tomatoes drained and cut up.
Sauté sausage and onion in a 12 inch Dutch oven over medium heat until onion is transparent. Add all remaining ingredients until except tomatoes. Bring to a boil, reduce heat, cover and simmer for 25 minutes or until vegetables are tender. Stir in tomatoes and simmer for 5 minutes more. Should serve 6 to 8 people.

THANKS FOR SHARING JOHN

*** Something for Everyone Stew

1 ½ lbs. of beef, pork, lamb or chicken
cut into bite size chunks
Vegetables of your choice
1 carrot, ½ onion, 1 potato, 1 stalk of celery, & etc. per person
1 can spiced tomato juice cocktail, large per every 6 people
4 tbsp. tapioca per 6 person.

Warm and oil a 12 inch deep Dutch oven. Layer meat and then the vegetables in the oven. Combine the juice and tapioca, mix well. Pour over the layers and bake slow in a medium oven 325 degrees. In your Volcano on 10 briquettes for 2 hrs. With briquettes only, 10 on the bottom and 10 on top. Replace when needed. In your oven, 325 for 2 hours. You can be very creative with this one.

To keep rust from forming between your cast iron skillets, place a paper towel between each pan before storing. The towels absorb the moisture.

*** Grandma Louisa's bean Soup

Bring to a simmering boil, 2 c beans (any style), 2 potato's, 1 medium chopped onion and 3 carrots cut up . Cook for 2 hours slowly keeping the water just above the mix. Add 2 cups
of broken spaghetti noodles and 1 tsp. salt and ½ tsp. pepper. Cook until noodles
are soft and serve.

From my Great Grandmother -

*** Rhubarb Pudding

Butter thin slices of dry bread, lay in bottom of a warmed and oiled 12 inch Dutch Oven. Put a layer of finely chopped Rhubard on top of the bread. Sprinkle with 1 cup brown sugar. Now repeat the layers of bread, Rhubard and sugar. Finish with a layer of bread. Pour ½ cup cream over the top, Cover and bake for 30 minutes at 350. In your Volcano, 12 briquettes, and 10 on the bottom and 15 on top with briquettes only

Yummy Yummy"

*** Cherry Almond Nut Rolls

Warm and oil a 12 Dutch Oven, Place 12 Rhodes bake and serve rolls of White, Wheat or Honey Wheat in the oven. Brush the tops with melted butter. Allow them to double in size. Take a spoon and dip in melted butter. Make a well in the top of each roll. Place a spoonful of Cherry pie filling in each roll. Drop a few slivered almonds on cherries. Bake for 20 minutes on 12 coals in your Volcano. 20 minutes on 375 in your oven at home. Use 15 on top and 10 on the bottom in the open camp site. While rolls are baking prepare 1 ½ cups powdered sugar 3 tbsp. cream or milk. Drizzle frosting over rolls when done and sprinkle on a few more almonds.

*** Is it Really that good , Cowboy Sweet potatoes.

Mash 4 already peeled cooked sweet potatoes. Add 1 8 oz can of crushed pineapple and 2 tbsp butter, salt and pepper, mix well. Flatten in the Dutch Oven. Combine ½ cup crushed saltines or Ritz crackers. 2 tbsp. Brown sugar, ¼ tsp cloves and 2 tbsp. butter. Sprinkle over potato mixture, in your Dutch Oven. Bake for 30 minutes In your Volcano, use 10 briquettes, in your oven 350 degrees and with briquettes only,

*** Apple Pancakes

Make pancakes from the master mix on page 71 To the pancakes, add 1 cup of grated apples and ½ tsp. cinnamon. Stir to mix, and cook as you would regular pancakes. If you have a diabetic or dieter, serve unsweetened applesauce instead of syrup.

*** Apple Waffles

Mix recipe from master mix on page 71, and use milk instead of water to mix. Also eliminate oil and use melted butter. Add 1 tbsp. brown sugar, ½ tsp. salt, 1 cup grated apples and 1 tsp. cinnamon. Mix together and cook in cast iron waffle iron if available or your waffle iron at home. Can also be cooked as a pancake.

"Don't forget to brush your tooth"

*** Bread Pudding.

2 cups dry bread (broken up, left over sweet rolls or toast.   4 cup milk
4 eggs-----------1/2 cup sugar------------1 tsp. vanilla--------1/4 tsp. salt
½ cup raisins.
Beat together milk, eggs, sugar and Vanilla, raisins and salt. Pour over bread or what ever you are using Pour in a warmed and oiled 10 inch Dutch Oven. Sprinkle a little Nutmeg over the pudding, and bake for 1 hour or when a knife inserted comes out clean. Lemon sauce, whipped cream or half and half can be served with this dish. Warm or cold its a great dish. 10 briquettes in you Volcano, and be sure not to put any heat in the center of the over on the bottom. 8 bottom and 12 top if briquettes only. In your oven at home, 350 for 1 hour.
On your Log Cabin Dutch Oven stove, 10 bottom and 10 top . The smell will tell you when it is done.

Remember the only way to dry your Dutch Oven is to Heat it up .

Western 4 - Bean Chili

1 can each, Black Beans, Pinto Beans, White Northern,
and Red Kidney Beans
1 red and 1 green pepper chopped
1 medium onion chopped
½ cup dry red wine
1 can chopped stewed tomatoes
4 tsp. chili powder,--- 2 tsp. sugar
½ tsp Real Salt----------1/2 tsp. white or black pepper
1 tsp. each, --basil, garlic powder, oregano and cumin

2 lbs. of hamburger can be cooked with the spices,
or 3 cups cooked chicken.

In a warmed and oiled 12 inch Dutch oven, sauté onions 'peppers, salt, pepper and spices. Simmer for 5 minutes and add remaining ingredients. Bring to a boil and place the lid on the pot. Allow to simmer for 15 minutes reducing the heat on the bottom. Garnish the chili with shredded cheese and onions. Should make approximately 8 to 10 servings.

*** Gene Autry Texas Chili

In a 12 inch warmed and oiled Dutch oven, cook 1 ½ lbs. hamburger, 1 tbsp garlic, 1 med. Onion, chopped, 1 chopped green pepper. Add 1 bottle chili sauce, 1 can kidney beans, 1 large can stewed tomatoes, Simmer for 30 minutes and add 1 cup grated jack cheese. Just before serving and top with chopped onions and yellow cheese.

Page 77

*** Green Bean and Meat Balls

2 lbs. hamburger
¼ cup flour
1 medium onion chopped
1 tsp. Real salt
½ tsp celery salt and pepper
3 cans green beans, drained
1 envelope onion soup mix.
2 cans cream of mushroom soup
2 cups sour cream   1 cup water

Make meat balls out of the first 5 ingredients and roll in flour. Place in the warmed and oiled 12 inch Dutch oven.
Place the lid on and cook for 15 minutes Place all other ingredients in the pot and simmer for 30 minutes at 350.
That's 12 briquettes in your Volcano, 10 on the bottom and 15 on top for briquettes only, replacing as necessary.
350 in your oven at home and 12 briquettes in your Log Cabin Dutch oven stove.

**Remember that if you use good briquettes such as Kingsford you can maintain a closer control on your
temperatures. Kinsgsford burns hotter longer and with a more even heat than any other briquette on the
market Cooking with wood is a real challenge because some wood burns hotter such as cedar.
The mastery of Dutch oven cooking, does include cooking over a camp fire. The easiest
way is to cook in your oven at home.**

*** Beef Stroganoff

The beef stroganoff as we know it today, was invented by Serge Stroganoff, a court cook in the reign of Catherine the Great of Russia. She was a cruel despot but encouraged the cooks of her time to adopt the French cooking methods to create new dishes. Today's stroganoff is a mild imitation of those years. The recipes of today are not much more than sour cream mixed in brown gravy. The original recipe had no sour cream in it.

3 tbsp. butter
3 tbsp. chopped onion
1 tbsp. flour
1 ½ cup beef soup broth
1 cup sour buttermilk
2 lbs. thin sliced beef stew meat
¼ tsp. black pepper
½ tsp Real salt

Melt the butter in a 12 inch Dutch oven with the onions and the meat. Simmer over a medium fire until the meat is done. Salt and pepper. Make a sauce as follows, 2 tbsp. butter in a fry pan until it starts to turn brown. Take from the fire and add 1 ¾ tbsp. of flour into the hot butter until the mixture forms a syrupy consistency not a thick paste. Add more butter if necessary. Now add 1 ½ cups beef broth . Now place back on the stove and bring back to a boil. Stir constantly Now add buttermilk and stir well. Be sure to use Sour buttermilk not sour cream. Now pour the meat sauce into the gravy sauce. Now serve with Buttered rice or noodles, Mashed potatoes or over toast.

- **To sour buttermilk, leave in a bowl at room temperature until it thickens.**

Page 79

*** Skillet Corn Bread

2 tbsp. stone ground cornmeal
2 cups self rising cornmeal mix
1 tsp. Real salt
1 egg 2 cups buttermilk

Warm and oil a 12 inch Dutch oven. Or in your home use a 12" fry pan. Sprinkle the stone ground meal in the bottom of the pan. Mix the remaining ingredients and pour into the pan. Bake 30 minutes over 12 briquettes in your volcano or Log Cabin stove. In your oven bake at 350 for 30 minutes. For briquettes only, 10 on the bottom and 15 on top. Replace as needed to maintain heat.

The lightening bug is brilliant, but he hasn't any mind.
He fluttered through existence with his headlight on behind.

*** Corn Dogs

Mix together, 2/3 cup cornmeal, 1 cup flour, 1 ½ tsp. baking powder, 1 tsp. Real salt and 2 tbsp. sugar. Cut 3 tbsp. of butter into this mixture. Add 1 egg and ¾ cup milk. Mix only enough to blend. Rinse and pat dry 8 to 10 hot dogs. Dip into meal mix and fry until golden brown in 2 to 3 inches of hot oil. Can also be fried in a fry pan if desired.

Add 2 Tbsp. of chopped onion and 1 tsp. dry mustard for a variety.

Kids Camping Section
and Miscellaneous

At one time or another, preferably when you are young, you learn something about cooking over a camp fire. It is such a great experience that I hope everyone tries it at least once. There is something special about sitting around a campfire with good friends, family and great conversation. A special campfire program can make a memory last for a lifetime. Sometimes it's what you cook or songs you sing or topics you talk about that makes the memory. What ever works for you, use it often. Some special dish you cook up or a fun thing to do like caramel corn or fry bread can make a big difference. Try making crackers or marshmallows, Roasting dipped vegetables, or doing shis-kabobs. There is so many things to do that I decided to share some of the things my family enjoyed and things I learned in Scouting.

When going on a camp trip whether in your back yard, a park, a state park, national park, unimproved camp areas or wilderness areas, practice your No Trace Camping. Pack it in, Pack it out. Leave No Trace, Tread Lightly or what ever you call it. Take care of the land we have been blessed with, so that others, after us, can enjoy it also.

If your ever up around the Missoula Montana area, drop into the **NINE-MILE Historic Ranger Station** at Huson Montana and see their displays on No Trace. Camping Ask questions of any Forest service personnel and if they don't know the answer, they will find it for you. Look at the Mule team they use to teach us how to pack in the Back wilderness area's, and walk thru the barns and buildings see the way they fight the fires in or back country. It's a great part of our history. Learn about the real Smokey Bear and Woodsy Owl.
See how fire Jumpers and fighters are trained and why they are so important to our forests.
Say HI to the crew and enjoy their friendship. Only each of us, can keep our country
clean and safe for the future.

*** Here's a Bit of History

In the early 1900's, Henry Ford who hated to be wasteful, gets the credit for designing and producing today's briquettes. He owned a sawmill in Michigan that made the wooden frames for his model T's. He was frustrated with the growing piles of wood chips and decided to chip the wood into small pieces and convert it to charcoal. It would then be ground into charcoal and compressed into what we know today as the pillow shaped briquettes. These convenient briquettes were sold thru Ford automobile agencies. Ford eventually put his brother in law, E.G. Kingsford in charge of the briquette charcoal operation. Together they helped to make barbecuing what it is today. An American tradition. It was originally called Ford charcoal, but later renamed Kingsford charcoal Briquettes. It was the original briquette and today still the best on the market. These briquettes light faster, last longer and give a more even heat. Kingsford Briquettes with the Volcano, and the Log Cabin Stove just form a perfect union. The charcoal lights in 6 to 10 minutes and cooks with a more even heat. Charcoal also offers a safe storage fuel. Store them in the bag they came, in up off the cement floor or ground and they will last a long time.

Start Your own
*** Family Traditions;

Hold high your family values and traditions. The reason our nation is still free and independent is because we learned to work for what we have, and to preserve the past as a remembrance as to how we got here. Take time to record in writing the things you do and enjoy. Teach your children to be grateful for what you have and earn what it is they want for the future. Learn to create things for future generations to keep as treasures. Not every thing can be bought. Our government is not responsible for our happiness and wealth. " We are". I'm not a politician, but I am a mother and love the world we have to live in. Our government was founded on "**GOD and his principles**" but we have lost sight of what our fore-fathers gave us. Give your family, photo albums with written inscriptions and places to remember. Live your life as though someone was going to write a history of it. " If you want to have bread, you can't loaf. "
Record recipes, Share your heritage, preserve pictures, identify heirlooms, and give memories.

*** Everybody's Favorite, Prime Rib

1 5 or 6 lb. Rib roast
1 tbsp. garlic salt
½ tsp. pepper
1 tbsp. Log cabin seasoning
Apple Cider Vinegar and water mixture
5 lbs. rock salt (water softener salt will do).

Guess what I had to give up for you.

      In a 12 inch deep Dutch oven, after it has been warmed and lightly oiled, cover the bottom with about ½ inch rock salt. If you want to, place a trivet on the salt and place roast on it with the bones down. Spray with vinegar water or moisten with water. Remember that vinegar is a tenderizer and will not effect the taste. Sprinkle on seasonings, and completely cover with remaining salt. This will form a cavity over the roast and act as a double oven while baking. Cover the pot with lid and bake 12 briquettes in your Volcano, 10 on the bottom and 15 on top with briquettes only or your Log Cabin pot belly stove. In your oven at home bake 350 for 2 ½ hours or until you can smell it. The smell will definitely tell you when it is done. Figure a ½ lb. Of meat per person unless you are really a Prime rib lover. Remove lid and crack away the salt. Brush off the excess and serve.

What travels around the world but stays in a corner---------a stamp
What are the six main seasons---------------------------------- Summer - Winter - Spring, Fall, Salt and Pepper.
See how many words you can make from the work camping ?? Pam Map and etc.

*** A Welch Recipe   "Caws Pobi"

This recipe was given to me by a dear sweet sister in law who went back to England and brought it to me. He r name is Nancy Dowson Moss. She lives in Riverton, Wyo. And you've never seen a more active woman `"` *She bowl's in the senior Olympics, swims, Line Dances and walks a lot. As of this year 1998 she's 76. She's a great neighbor too.* `'`

3 slices bread your choice
¼ cup grated cheese
6 tbsp. milk
2 tbsp. butter
Real salt and pepper to taste
Mustard if desired

I would call it " CHEESE BREAKFAST TOAST "
Serve with fresh sliced tomatoes if possible.

This one's a great treat

Slowly melt the cheese, butter and milk in a saucepan or 8 inch Dutch Oven. Add butter salt and mustard as desired. When piping hot, pour over the toast. A little beer can be added to the mixture, and it can be browned under a broiler if desired. When camping, it can be browned on a griddle or fry pan as you would French Toast.

***** HOW TO TREAD LIGHTLY*****

1. **Avoid** running over trees, brush shrubs and grasses, damaging or killing them.
2. **Stay** off soft wet roads and trails readily torn up by vehicles. Especially during hunting season.
3. **Travel** around meadows, steep hillsides or stream banks and lakeshores that will be easily scared.
4. **Resist** the urge to pioneer a new road or trail or cut across a switchback.
5. **Stay** away from animals rearing young.
6. **Obey** gate closure signs. Vandalism causes tax payers money and angers property owners.
7. **Stay out** of wilderness areas with your vehicle. Know where the boundaries are.
8. **Get Permission** to travel across private land.

*** Camping Fajitas

2 lbs. thin sliced or chopped beef
¾ cup beer optional
2 tbsp. Worcestershire sauce
2 each red and green peppers sliced
1 large onion sliced   ½ tsp. garlic powder
Real salt and pepper to taste.
1 regular can stewed tomatoes optional
1 heaping tsp. Log cabin or Volcano seasoning.

Jalapeno and Cilantro can be added if desired
¼ cup lime juice

It's so fun to do.

Combine all ingredients in a 12 inch fry pan or the bottom of a 12 inch Dutch oven. Sauté over the heat until desired doneness is obtained. Warm tortillas shells and serve with the Fajitas. Excellent for a quick campfire dish.

*** Barbecue Potatoes

6 to 8 potatoes
½ cup barbecue sauce any kind
¼ cup water
1 medium onion
1 tsp. Real salt and pepper

Wash and slice in half the potatoes. Warm and oil a 12 inch Dutch oven. Arrange the potatoes in the bottom.
Mix the water and barbecue sauce together, pour over the Potatoes. Arrange sliced onion on top and sprinkle 1 tsp. Real salt over the top . Pepper if desired.

Bake at 350 degrees at home, for 35 minutes, 12 briquettes in your Volcano, and 15 on top, 12 on the bottom for briquettes only and 12 in your Log Cabin stove, Bottom heat only.
This can be done in tin foil also on campfire.

Page 85

*** SKILLET SUPPERS

Your Grandmas skillet could be the original nonstick skillet if its cast-iron. When used frequently, cast iron takes on a rich, dark color and a non-stick finish. The cast iron pours take on a slick finish that seal the seasoning in and makes cooking in them a joy. Weight is a problem to some, but to those who know the benefits of cast, its an even heat, that browns without burning. **REMEMBER THE ONLY WAY TO DRY CAST IRON IS TO HEAT IT AND EVAPORATE THE MOISTURE FROM THE POURS.** Season your cast right the first time at 450 or 500 degrees.

*** PORK CHOP SKILLET MEAL

In a heated and oiled 12 inch skillet, brown your pork chops. You can flour them first if you wish. Now salt and pepper. Slice 1 large onion and place on top of Pork Chops. Pour on 1 can of cream of mushroom soup diluted. Simmer while you prepare 6 large potatoes quartered and 6 large carrots sliced in half. Add to the meat and soup and simmer for 1 hour or more until vegetables are tender. Be sure to cook low and slow or soup will scorch. Excellent supper and the chops are extremely tender.

*** BROCCOLI SKILLET CHICKEN

In a large cast-iron skillet, combine 4 tbsp. butter, 4 tbsp. flour and 2 cups milk to make a white sauce gravy. Stir until smooth and salt and pepper to taste. Add 2 cans cooked chicken and 2 to 3 cups broccoli. Simmer for 8 to 10 minutes and serve with rolls, toast of muffins. A small amount of onion salt and garlic can be added. Use your imagination and add canned carrots, white beans or what ever.

Challenge yourself to always leave a camp site cleaner than you found it. "So Easy to do"

EATING OUTDOORS
In the Woods-----Up in the Mountain-----At the Beach-----In a park-----In your own Backyard

*** Roasting Corn on a Campfire

1 ear of corn per person or more if desired (I can eat 2).
1 bottle of squeeze butter from the grocer   Real salt to taste
Pull the husk back and remove as much silk as possible. Replace husk and drop in cold water for 25 to 30 minutes.

Totally Awesome

*** Picnic Tricks

The trapper type of fire is the most useful of camp or picnic fires. Never start cooking until the wood has burned and settled to a bed of red, glowing coals. Place two medium sized logs about six or eight inches apart. Between them set up dried twigs and shavings. If weather has been wet, split dried logs for dry shavings. Light carefully using good tinder to start the fire. Birch and cedar bark are the best of natural tinder's. Adjust the logs to fit the cooking utensil or grill you brought. Smokeless cooking can be done best over beds of hardwood coals. Always take your own wood when possible. Gather only downed wood. Make your fire in already existing fire pits. Be sure that surrounding areas are free of dried grasses. Never build under live trees There are several different kinds of fires Below are a few ideas. Use the one that works best for you.

Page 87

*** Camp Tricks for Quick Breakfasts ***

Breakfast in the open is probably the best meal. The morning peacefulness, the sun peaking over the morning and another day to spend your life. Thank you lord for letting us wake up another morning.

*** Egg in a Poke

For a quick breakfast, tear a hole in a slice of bread. Warm and oil a 12 inch Dutch or fry pan or griddle. Lightly butter the bread and place in the fry pan. Break an egg in the hole Fry until cooked on one side and flip over. Serve with syrup or jelly.

*** Hunters Biscuits

One handful of flour, two fingers of baking powder, pinch of salt, piece of butter the size of your thumb. Mix well and add enough milk to make a soft dough. Cook biscuits 8 minutes on each side in a lightly buttered frying pan, at a moderate heat. You can also bake in an 8 inch Dutch Oven or a reflector oven as described on later pages.

Scrambled Eggs and Cheese

Beat 8 eggs and ½ cup milk well and add ¾ tsp. salt and ¼ tsp pepper. Melt 4 tbsp. butter in a fry pan and pour in the eggs. Stir well until eggs begin to thicken. Slowly add 1 cup american cheese. Serve on toast. Be careful not to over cook.

When breaking camp, always put your fire completely out. Use soil and water. Test to see if the fire is completely out. Use your bare hands. The slightest coal can start up again with a small wind. Dig a hole for your fire if it is windy day or use a Volcano. Don't forget that forest fires take away the homes of animals and destroy many beautiful things.

*** Fun In The Winter

Right around Christmas time, when your days are really your own, there's something about the frosty invitation of a world wrapped in winter that makes you catch your breath. The magnitude of a white shrouded landscape, the almost brittle quality of cloudless days, the grandeur of the sun claiming his few short hours. There is no resisting it. Whether you walk out into the open or travel hundreds of miles to your winter sport, you'll be glad you went. There's a favorite winter stunt you will want to try next time you're out during a fresh snow storm. Gather up some clean fluffy snow and make a big batch of SNOW ICE CREAM. It's just this easy. Sprinkle granulated sugar over the top of the fresh snow and stir. Add milk a little at a time, more sugar, Vanilla, and stir again. Until it is the consistency of ice cream. Taste it as you go to see if it has enough sugar and vanilla. Serve it with fudge sauce or cocoa and cookies for a substantial contribution to insatiable winter appetites.

*** Campfire Bananas

4 bananas
2 milk chocolate candy bars
½ cup miniature marshmallows

Peel back one section of the banana peel but don't remove it. Slice across the banana in one inch pieces. Remove every other piece. Fill holes with chocolate and marshmallows. Close up the banana and wrap in tin foil. Place in the camp fire or on a grill over the camp fire. Let bananas rest in or over the fire for about 8 to 10 minutes. Marshmallows should be melted.

Page 89

*** Teriyaki Pork Chops

1/2 cup soy sauce
¼ cup oil
1 medium onion chopped fine
1/3 cup honey
¼ cup red wine
4 tsp. ginger
1 tbsp. garlic
8 pork chops

Marinate pork chops in all of the ingredients over night. Place in a 12 inch Dutch oven with the marinade and cover. Cook for 1 hour over 12 briquettes in your Volcano or 10 on the bottom and 15 on top with briquettes only. These can also be grilled over your briquettes also. Cook and turn often, marinating with the sauce each time you turn.

*** Cajun Fish

Before you go camping, combine 2 tsp. paprika 21 tsp. salt, 2 tsp. onion powder, 2 tsp. garlic powder, 1 tsp. cayenne pepper, 1 ½ tsp. white and black pepper, 1 tsp. thyme and 1 tsp. oregano. Place in a zip lock baggy, and take with you in case you catch a fish. Melt butter and coat fish fillet. Coat with seasoning and fry. This will work on any fish. Cut back on peppers if you do not like the spicy seasoning.

Pledge to Tread Lightly by traveling only where motorized vehicles are permitted.
Remain on trails that are designated for foot travel.

BUCKET STOVE

**CIRCULAR TIN CAN OVEN
WITH HINGED LID**

• Prepare a green stick to act as a skewer by removing the bark from the end on which the food is to go (the thinnest end) and sealing it by placing over the hot embers briefly.

Shish Kebabs

• Thread the ingredients, as desired, onto the stick and place it over glowing embers. Turn occasionally. It is advisable to manufacture some form of support at either end of the skewer in order to keep it in position—and to prevent your hands getting burned!

Broiled Fish

There are alternative methods to pan and pot cooking, above are a few to try.

Page 91

Some Traditional Camp Gadgets

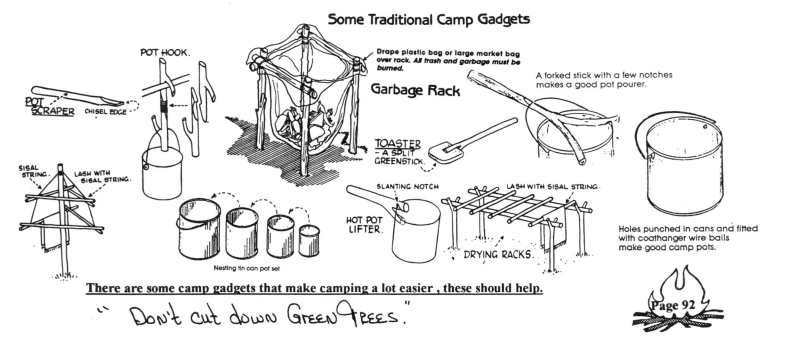

POT HOOK.

POT SCRAPER CHISEL EDGE

Drape plastic bag or large market bag over rack. *All trash and garbage must be burned.*

Garbage Rack

A forked stick with a few notches makes a good pot pourer.

SISAL STRING. LASH WITH SISAL STRING.

TOASTER – A SPLIT GREENSTICK.

SLANTING NOTCH

HOT POT LIFTER.

LASH WITH SISAL STRING.

DRYING RACKS.

Nesting tin can pot set

Holes punched in cans and fitted with coathanger wire bails make good camp pots.

There are some camp gadgets that make camping a lot easier , these should help.

" Don't cut down Green Trees."

Page 92

THINGS TO MAKE FOR CAMPING

WINTER GROUND BED

-SNOW-
SLEEPING BAG W/EXTRA BLANKET
FOAM PAD
SPACE BLANKET
GROUND CLOTH
NEWSPAPERS
LEAVES-PINE BOUGHS
-SNOW-
-SNOW-
-SNOW-

Building a Winter Ground Bed

To build a winter ground bed, first either clear away or pack down any snow that may cover the ground. Then build several layers of insulation between you and the ground. Remember, in really cold weather, snow itself can be an insulation against severe cold. The illustration depicts several suggested layers of insulation that form a ground bed.

Extra blankets inside a sleeping bag can help, as can fresh long underwear donned just before climbing into the sack. A stocking cap or a hooded sweatshirt will help keep heat from escaping from your body through the top of your head.

hose, ¼-½ inch in diameter. Insert a 10- to 12-inch length of metal tubing into one end.

Now simply point where you want the "wind" and blow. While this may hurt the old gag about sending a young Scout to get a left-handed smoke shifter, it can be used to backfire on a wiseacre older Scout.

Odds and Ends

Learn about camp layouts and proper disposal and storage of food. Especially if your in bear country

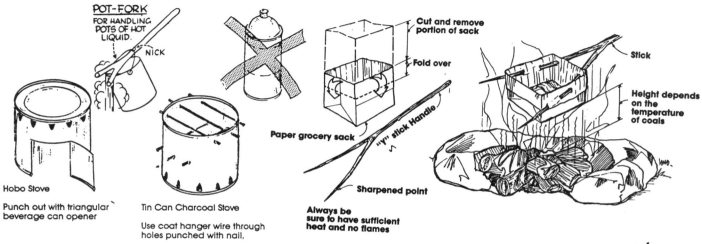

POT-FORK
FOR HANDLING POTS OF HOT LIQUID.

NICK

Cut and remove portion of sack

Fold over

Stick

Height depends on the temperature of coals

Paper grocery sack

"Y" stick Handle

Hobo Stove

Punch out with triangular beverage can opener

Tin Can Charcoal Stove

Use coat hanger wire through holes punched with nail.

Sharpened point

Always be sure to have sufficient heat and no flames

Remember to know your area and not cut down living trees. When you take a trees life, you should always replace it by planting two back.

Page 94

COOKIE PAN REFLECTOR OVEN

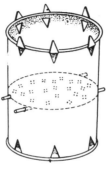

Two cookie pans about ¼-inch deep

Smaller pan as deep as required for baking

Tin strip length of ¼-inch pans

Three rods 2 inches longer than pans

Two pieces tin for ends

Holes for rods

Twenty-two paper fasteners

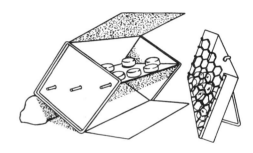

To save charcoal, put a grate in your stove.

BREAKFAST OVER HOT COALS USING PAPER GOODS

Here's a good reflector oven for baking. The heat comes from burning charcoal in a shallow bake pan. Chicken wire holds charcoal in place.

Page 95

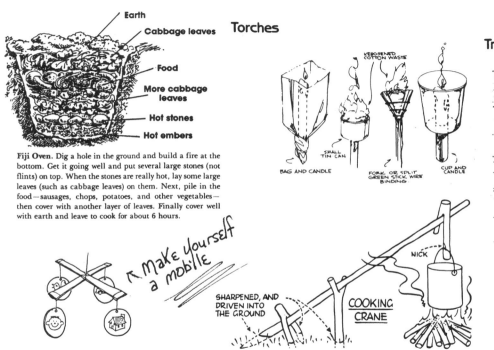

Fiji Oven. Dig a hole in the ground and build a fire at the bottom. Get it going well and put several large stones (not flints) on top. When the stones are really hot, lay some large leaves (such as cabbage leaves) on them. Next, pile in the food—sausages, chops, potatoes, and other vegetables—then cover with another layer of leaves. Finally cover well with earth and leave to cook for about 6 hours.

- Earth
- Cabbage leaves
- Food
- More cabbage leaves
- Hot stones
- Hot embers

Torches

KEROSENED COTTON WASTE

SMALL TIN CAN

BAG AND CANDLE

FORK OR SPLIT GREEN STICK WIRE BINDING

CUP AND CANDLE

← make yourself a mobile

COOKING CRANE

SHARPENED, AND DRIVEN INTO THE GROUND

NICK

Tree "Fridge"

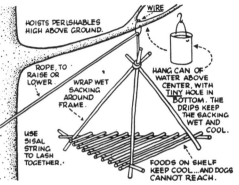

WIRE

HOISTS PERISHABLES HIGH ABOVE GROUND.

ROPE, TO RAISE OR LOWER

WRAP WET SACKING AROUND FRAME.

USE SISAL STRING TO LASH TOGETHER.

HANG CAN OF WATER ABOVE CENTER, WITH TINY HOLE IN BOTTOM. THE DRIPS KEEP THE SACKING WET AND COOL.

FOODS ON SHELF KEEP COOL...AND DOGS CANNOT REACH.

Box Oven Baking

Box oven cakes are fun to make and delicious to eat in the out-of-doors. You don't need to wait for a special occasion to make one.

Materials

Cardboard box, approximately 12" x 16" x 14" deep for large cake; 12" square for smaller cake.

Aluminum foil

Scotch or masking tape

Knife

4 to 6 empty 12-oz beverage cans

Charcoal

Plastic roasting wrap (optional)

Cake pan

Cake mix and/or ingredients

Canned frosting

Decorator frosting with fancy tip, tube or push-button can

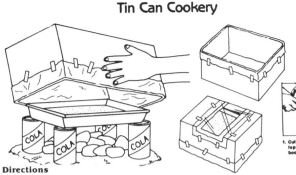

Directions

For a 9-inch by 13-inch cake, cut the top flaps off a large box. Line the inside of the box with aluminum foil, bringing the foil around the edges and down the outer side about 4 inches. Anchor with tape. If you want to watch what is happening in your oven, cut a square hole in the solid top of the oven box, and tape clear plastic roasting wrap tightly over the hole.

Fill four empty beverage cans about half full with sand or dirt, and place them in the charcoal pit so each can will support a corner of your cake pan.

Light 14 pieces of charcoal; then mix your cake.

When the charcoal is giving off even heat, spread the coals, set cake pan on the beverage cans, and place cardboard! box oven over the pan. Make a small gap for air at each end of the oven by scraping some dirt away. Air circulation is needed to keep the charcoal burning.

Bake cake for the length of time specified in the recipe. Do not peek! Lifting the box will cause the oven to lose heat.

If you use an 8-inch square pan and a 12-inch square box for the oven, light only 12 pieces of charcoal.

Fun night time Activity

1. Cut a 3"x3" opening in the box top, slides fit grooves in side-boards.

2. Assembled box is 12" long, 6½" square inside ends. Top fits snugly.

3. Make star cards on heavy paper by punching out all the constellations.

4. Slip star card in place. Experiment to get best angle for the flashlight.

5. Two flashlight holders keep light source steady for projecting the stars.

Each constellation is laid out on heavy paper in accordance with the diagram given in any book on astronomy. Punch a hole at each star location, trying to make holes larger or smaller as indicated on the relative brightness charts in your source book. The edges of the holes should be smooth so that the light beam can go through evenly. A high-speed drill with a ¼" bit helps to make clean holes in thick paper.

The completed star-gazing box can be decorated by covering it with heavy wrapping paper on which you have drawn a variety of constellations or horoscope signs with India ink.

"Need a good flash light"

Page 97

creative   campfires

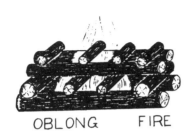

OBLONG   FIRE

MODEL FIREPLACE

Tin lid (painted)

Dowel

Matches

Campfires and Lighting

Start fire here

TOP LIGHTER FIRE

"Your can cook alot on these fires"

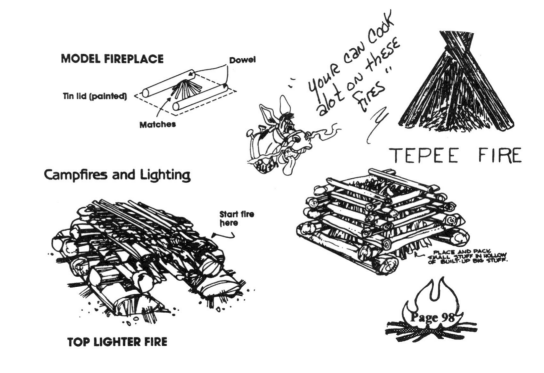

TEPEE FIRE

PLACE AND PACK SMALL STUFF IN HOLLOW OF BUILT-UP BIG STUFF.

Page 98

*** Black Bean Chili Nachos

In a 12 inch cast-iron skillet, sauté 1 lb. Hamburger and ½ lb. Sausage with 1 medium onion chopped with 2 tbsp. oil. Add 1 tbsp. chili powder, 1 tbsp. ground cumin, ½ cup red and green peppers. Sauté until meat is done, and add 1 can black beans, drained , to the mixture. Stir in 1 can stewed tomatoes, and add 2 tbsp. chopped jalapeno if you like spicy. Chopped cilantro is optional also. Cook on a low simmer for 15 minutes, and spoon over the top of chips. Sprinkle grated cheese over the nachos and serve. Black olives can also be added to the chips. Great in the out of doors.

*** Barbecued Bacon Franks
Slit a hot dog length wise, and place a cheese stick in the center. Wrap each frank with a couple strips of bacon and secure with toothpicks. Place on a hot dog stick and barbecue over coals. Serve with relish and ketchup in a hot dog bun or eat it plain. Great for kids.

*** Pickle Dog
Shape a seasoned hamburger patty around your favorite kind of pickle. Wrap with bacon strips and secure with toothpicks. Broil, grill or roast over an open fire. Serve on a hot dog bun with your favorite garnish.

*** Hobo Dinner
Wrap in a double piece of tin foil, a hamburger patty, 1 sliced carrot, 1 sliced potato 1 slice of onion with salt and pepper to taste. Seal foil and wrap again. Cook over campfire or on a barbecue grill, turning often.
Remember to ask permission to enter private land. Always close gates behind you.

*** Corn Dogs
(with or without sticks)

Boil hot dogs in water. Mix batter and fry in deep fat hot oil until golden brown.
Batter;

2 eggs	¾ tsp. salt
¼ cup sugar	2 tsp. baking powder
1 ¼ c. milk	1 c. corn meal
2 c. flour	

" Grown up kids like these too."

Mix all ingredients together and dip hot dogs in. Sticks can be inserted in dogs as soon as they are hot.

*** Cracker Stuffing for Fish

1 ½ c. crushed crackers,------1 1/2 c. milk------1 tbsp. butter-----1 small onion chopped------1/2 c. chopped celery
1/8 tsp each, white pepper, nutmeg, and salt.   Mix crackers with seasonings and melted butter. Add milk and stir
until well blended. Place in fish and fry or bake in your Dutch oven.

**Plan your outings in advance. Know if you need a permit or can gather wood. Have a few games planned
for the family. Relay games are always fun for all ages. Contests for calling husbands, wives, members of
the family, and even hogs. People like to throw things too. Rolling pins, pie tins, marshmallows, cow chips,
hot dogs, paper plates, balloons, or just about anything. Consult any game book or make up your own.
Grandpa Nelson always had nickels for the winners or the sack race, three legged races or chicken or
duck walks. In my day, Lifesavers were a big prize. Mom always had a prize for the biggest
fish caught too.**

*** Camp Fire Sing Along

No body could sing or Yodel like my mom. But we all try every time we get together. Camp fires can be real fun.
Here's one for you. My brother Norman and his family love to sing too.

TOM THE TOAD (*Oh Christmas Tree*)

Oh Tom the toad, oh Tom the toad, why are you lying in the road
Repeat first line
You did not see the car ahead and on your head is tire treads
Oh Tom the toad , Oh Tom the toad , why are you lying in the road.

Oh Matt the rat, Oh Matt the rat, why did you tease my pussycat
Repeat first line
You used to be so brown and thin, and now you are inside of him
Oh Matt the rat, Oh Matt the rat, why did you tease my pussy cat.

Oh Doug the bug, Oh Doug the bug, why did you fall into my rug.
Repeat line
I really like to play with you, and now your stuck upon my shoe,
Oh Doug the bug, Oh Doug the bug, why did you fall into the rug.
Let your kids make up their own verses. Its a lot of fun to see what they come up with.

What do you call a man who raises giant honeybees.
A big bzzzzzz ness man.

Soup-Can Lanterns — Fill an empty tin can with sand or fill it with water and freeze it until the water becomes solid. This will allow you to work on the can without bending the metal. Put the can on a solid surface, and carefully using hammer and nail, make a design of holes around the sides of the can. Clean out the sand or ice, insert a coat hanger through the holes for hanging, and place a candle inside to finish the lantern. (See drawing.)

Fun to make

Page 101

*** Cooking on the Rocks

Cooking on the rocks is liken unto Dutch Oven cooking. You can't do it just once and expect to be an expert. You have to keep trying. Here are some tips to help.

1. Don't place cold stone in a hot fire. Some type of rock will explode. Build the fire over your cooking rocks, and let it burn down. Brush coals off and keep fire around the rocks to keep them hot.
2. Meats will cook a lot better if you slice it in thin pieces. Chicken, pork, beef, venison, elk and etc.
3. Clean the rocks by spraying with a water vinegar solution. You won't need much oil, and peanut oil will be best because it has a higher flash back point.
4. Biscuits bake up nicely on hot rocks. Easy to make an easy to serve. Ash cakes were a favorite of the mountain men.
5. Potatoes can be cooked on the rocks or in the fire.
6. Use ½ of and orange peel to cook your cake batter in or line with thin sliced ham and beaten eggs. It will bake nicely in a campfire.
7. Bacon can be fried up nicely on your hot rocks and served on a sandwich.

TRY IT< YOU"LL LIKE IT>

A Fun way to cook - Vinegar water is a good way to clean your rocks

Did you hear about the disturbance in the medicine cabinet ?? No, what happened. The baby aspirin cried and woke up the sleeping pills.

How do you stop a charging rhinoceros ?? Take away his credit cards.

What's another name for a Hospital ??? The halls of I.V.

" The Wok "

The favorite cooking utensil of the Chinese Chefs

The Chinese people have been using cast-iron for over 4000 years. Stir fry has been a favorite and specialty in that country for many years. The **Texsport cast-iron** is not a new product, just a new item for this Sporting goods company out of Texas. I highly recommend that you cook in cast-iron and learn the benefits and secrets of this type of cooking.

This is a quick camp stir-fry.
*** Hot Dog Stir-Fry

1 pkg. hot dogs
2 potatoes cut in ½ and sliced
1 med. Onion sliced
1 cup mushrooms sliced
1 cup celery chopped

Make Tuna Boat Sandwiches for a Summer Picnic — Mix one can of tuna fish with ½ cup mayonnaise. Fill both halves of a hot dog bun with tuna mixture. Cut a cheese slice diagonally and weave a toothpick through each piece. Insert cheese "sails" on the tuna "boats." (See drawing.)

Heat and oil your wok, place all ingredients in and stir fry until warmed all the way thru. Sprinkle with Log Cabin or Volcano seasoning and stir enough to distribute the seasoning. This can be done in a 12 inch Dutch oven bottom also. Potatoes and onions will be translucent.

Now use your imagination and try some varieties of your own. Remember to cook other meats first to assure doneness and then add veggies.

*** Chicken Peanut Stir Fry

Heat and add 2 tbsp oil to your **Texsport** wok.
2 large boneless chicken breasts or thighs.
1 small onion sliced
½ cup pea pods
1 cup mushrooms sliced
½ cup teriyaki or stir fry sauce
½ cup unsalted peanuts
½ cup celery chopped
1small can water chestnuts

Go Bug Hunting —
Cut out the two opposite sides of a milk carton and slip the carton into a leg cut from a pair of old stockings. Add some leaves from nearby plants and a cotton ball sprinkled with water. Catch a caterpillar, fly, cricket, beetle, or moth and place the bug inside the "bug cage" milk carton. Secure the stocking with a twist-tie. Watch the bug for a while, then let it go (near where it was found).

Thinly slice the meat and sauté in the wok until almost cooked thru. Add all other ingredients except the sauce and peanuts. Stir to warm and partially cook thru. Onions will be transparent. Serve over cooked rice or noodles. Be sure to add the sauce just before you serve it This is a great dish for camping also and easy to prepare before hand.

Although most back country waters would pass the grade for bacterial count, it is not worth the chance you take to try it. A tiny microbe is enough to cause dysentery, and make your hiking experience miserable. The warnings on back country trail heads are true. All users who don't sterilize their waters are at risk of Giardiasis from contaminated water. Be prepared when you go to the back country. Don't be a victim of foolishness.

Toast Sunflower Seeds — Collect sunflower seeds from cultivated sunflowers and shell them. Spread shelled seeds in a single layer on a baking sheet and bake in a 350° degree oven for 5 minutes or toast in skillet on top of the stove over moderate heat. They make great snacks.

*** Hoo Te Makem
*** Clouty Dumplins

Thought yo might enjoy this one if'n you can figure it out.

Mix half a poond of plain flour , haffa teaspoon bakin poodor, pincha salt an a quartor poond of shreddy suet aaltegithor, addin bits of caad wettor te gerra smooth doe. Put some flour on a bord an roll oot flat, inch or soo thick. Wsh an chop a leek an onion, biggun, an spred oot on the dough addin salt an peppor. Wet the edges an squash it aal in a baal. Wesh a dish clout in boily wettor, lay it out an covor wi flour. Stick the baal on it an tie the ends wi string. Boil in a potjie a boilin wettor for a couple of ooers. Serve wi boily beef. Gan bonkors for it they de.

*** HOO THEY GOT THE NAME ***

Named after their inventor, Ethel Clouty
*   By she wor a big lass*

<u>Potjie's are a south African pot sold by the crazy African from Vail Arizona</u>
<u>You can contact Paul Zway at 1-888-762-8208 or e-mail him</u> *at*
<u>ranger@azstarnet.com</u>

Page 105

*** Making Corn Beef

Did you ever wonder how they made that wonderful tasting beef.??
Let me give you Grandma Kelly's way.

Ingredients for 6 gallons
10 ozs. Sugar
2 ozs. Sodium nitrate (available from druggist)
½ oz. Sodium nitrate   "" " " "
3 lbs. salt
3 tsp. black pepper
1 tsp. cloves
6 bay leaves
12 tsp pickling spice
3 onions chopped fine
4 garlic chopped fine

Outdoor Scavenger Hunt — Give one copy
of the following list to each player:
   Find a rock shaped like a triangle.
   Find a rock round like a marble.
   Find a rock that is sparkly.
   Find a rock that has many points.
   Find a twig shaped like the letter *Y*.
   Find a leaf that's as big as your hand.
   Find some pine needles.
   Find two pinecones of different sizes.
   Find a feather.

Put all ingredients into a crock jar and add enough water to make 6 gallons. Ideal temperature for corning meat is about 38 to 40 degrees. Spring or fall is the best time In the winter, use a room in the root cellar but try not to freeze it. If you have to corn the meat at a higher temperature, add 1/3 again as much salt for every 15 degrees above 40. Place your meat in the liquid and if it bobs above the liquid place a plate on top to hold it under. Cover the crock and leave the meat for 15 days. Round steak or tougher cuts of meat are perfect for corning.
On the 5th and 10th day, stir the liquid and reverse the position of the meat. Add a cup of apple cider vinegar to the liquid on the 5th day to assure a tender corn.
This is also great for Elk, Moose, Antelope, Pork, Bear, Caribou, Wild birds and etc.
Stored in a cool place the meet will last for 2 to 3 months. (below 38 degrees)

*** Authentic Irish Corned Beef and Cabbage
Cook corned meat as follows;

Place the corned meat in a Dutch oven with a small amount of cold water in the bottom. Place 6 medium sized onions and 8 whole carrots around the meat. Cover and bake for 2 hours on a low moderate heat 300 degrees. Salt and pepper to taste. Add 3 or 4 small cabbage heads cut in half and return to fire covered for another ½ hour. This way you will not over cook the cabbage. This is a very popular recipe around the Irish people. This recipe was brought to Utah by Captain Charles Kelly and his family. My great grandmother Kelly was a great cook and it was a pleasure to eat at her table. She actually cooked this recipe once for Brigham Young and Lorenzo Snow in Brigham City, Utah. Her father, Charles Kelly, was very prominent in, Utah.

*** Cooking Birds in Clay
Here's another old one for you.

To cook a bird in clay, first clean out the bird. Now cut off the head and claws, and remove tail and wings. Coat bird with 1 inch of thick clay until bird is totally covered. Bury bird in coals of your camp fire until clay is bake hard as a rock. Remove from the fire and crack the clay open. Feathers and skin will adhere to the clay as you peel it off. The bird will be moist and tender and well cooked. When I tried this recipe it did not work real well for me and my scouts, but the bird was eatable and tender done. It works exactly the right way on fish, and if horse mint plants are around put a leaf in your fish. If you pluck your bird it works well to. Something to try in an emergency.

*** Barbecue Salt
Here's seasoning salt you can mix up on your own.
1 cup brown sugar-----------1 cup salt---------1/1/2 oz. Paprika
2 tbsp. pepper-----------------1 ½ tsp. Cayenne ----1/4 tsp. cinnamon
1 tbsp. garlic powder
Mix all ingredients together and place in a covered jar in refrigerator.
Rub on meat before frying.

"Cookin in a Bag"

*** Laramie Hotel Seasoning Salt
This recipe was used in the Laramie Cattleman's Hotel in the 1800's
4 oz. Celery salt-------2 oz garlic powder--------1/2 tsp. paprika
½ to 1 cup sugar------4 oz onion powder---------1/4 c. chili powder
1 tbsp. pepper
Mix together and add to 2 ½ lb. Salt. This can be used for meats like
beef, pork, elk, lamb, or venison.

*** Brown Bag Biscuits
Saturate the bottom and sides of a brown paper bag with cooking oil. Place prepared biscuits in the bottom and
heat hanging over a camp fire. Bag should hang high enough not to burn but low enough to get good heat.

*** Egg on a Stick
Pierce small holes in egg and pass stick through egg. Heat over coals. Be sure that the stick is from a
nonpoisonous plant. Avoid holly, elm, yew or laurel.

All these recipes cook very well in the Log Cabin Stove or the Volcano.

Page 108

*** Egg in an Orange

Cut orange in half and remove the fruit. Save to eat later with meal. Place a thin slice of ham in the peel. Break egg in, and salt and pepper. Put in coals and cook. Egg can be scrambled ahead of time if desired. Add some flavored bread crumbs to make the eggs go farther.

*** Paper Cup Rice

Place ½ cup rice in a cup full of water. Seal the top with aluminum foil and place close to the coals but not directly on them. Us unlined, unwaxed cups. for best results.

*** Hot Dog Shish-Kabob

Alternate any of the following items on a 1, 2, or 3 prong hot dog stick. Sliced potatoes, folded pieces of ½ slices bacon, cut up hotdogs, mushrooms, cherry tomatoes, cooked chunks of beef or pork, mushrooms, pieces of onions or etc. Let your imagination do the work Can be a lot of fun.

*** Fillet of fish on a Hot Dog Stick.

Cut off the head and tail of the fish. Clean the fish properly and put lemon pepper, barbecue sauce onions or what ever inside. Work the wire stick or strong coat hanger thru the fish. You can remove the skin if you like, but I prefer to keep it on to hold the meat in place. You can weave green willows to hold the fish and cook over the camp fire. Picture below.

Paper-Plate Puppets — Tape or staple the rims of two paper plates together. On one plate, paint a face and use yarn, cloth, or crepe paper for hair and a hat. Cut a slit in the back plate to slip in your hand to hold the puppet. (See drawing.)

*** Taco Pie ALA Dutch Oven
For this you need a 10 and 12 inch.
INGREDIENTS:

1 lb. Hamburger---------1/3 cup olives
1 pkg. taco mix-----------1/3 cup water
1 c. sour cream   1 c. cheese
pkg. corn chips-----------1 can crescent dinner rolls
1 chopped medium onion, green and red pepper
METHOD:

"Fun to make"
Good to Eat

In a 10 inch Dutch oven or a skillet, brown hamburger, onion and peppers. Add olives, and taco seasoning diluted with water. Cover and let simmer. Meanwhile, warm and oil a 12 inch Dutch oven. Put crescent dinner rolls in bottom of Dutch over lapping until all used up. Crumble corn chips of your choice over the rolls. Add the hamburger mix, top with sour cream and sprinkle on grated cheese. White, yellow or mixed. Bake for 15 to 20 minutes covered. Great with green salad.
Pie crust, pizza crust, or bread crust can be used.

**** Bean Chowder
In a 12 inch deep Dutch oven, Sauté 1 lb. Hamburger or more, with 1 large chopped onion, 1 cup chopped celery, 1 chopped green pepper with 1 tsp. Real salt and ½ tsp. each of chili powder and thyme. Add 1 large can stewed tomatoes, 1 8oz can tomato sauce, 2 cups water, 2 bay leaves and ¼ tsp. pepper. Bring to a simmering boil and add 1 cup diced raw potatoes, 1 can kidney, black, red, pinto, garbanzo or what ever kind of beans. Dice and add 1 medium zucchini and 1 can whole can. Simmer until potatoes are tender, about 20 minutes with the lid on. Serve with parmesan cheese. And a roll or crackers or bread sticks.

"Thanks"
Colleen

Page 110

Collect Edible Plants — Gather cattails, purple violets, dandelions, spearmint, and berries from roadsides, fields, or gardens, with permission. Check cookbooks for recipes.